D1511521

THE STORY OF
AMERICAN RAILROADS

Books by Olive W. Burt

WIND BEFORE THE DAWN
I AM AN AMERICAN
OLD AMERICA COMES ALIVE
THE NATIONAL ROAD
JAYHAWKER JOHNNY
THE STORY OF AMERICAN RAILROADS

THE STORY OF
AMERICAN RAILROADS

And How They Helped Build a Nation

by OLIVE W. BURT

Illustrated

THE JOHN DAY COMPANY
New York

Library of Congress Catalogue Card Number: 77-76130

PRINTED IN THE UNITED STATES OF AMERICA

For Kate, who was so entranced with
her first train ride,
and
Amy, David, and Patty, for whom that
treat is still in store

ACKNOWLEDGMENTS

The very real concern of interested people in the situation of today's railroads and their possible future was shown by the prompt and generous assistance given by every railroad company, historical society, and library contacted during the preparation of this book. Special mention should be made of the help afforded by Douglas R. Stephenson and others of the Association of American Railroads; Edwin C. Schafer of the Union Pacific Railroad; John L. Stover, Southern Railway System; William B. Johnson, Illinois Central Railroad; C. F. Lane, United Transportation Union; and Miss Frances Duck, Stevens Institute of Technology.

CONTENTS

1

THE DREAMERS AND THEIR DREAM

Soon after the end of the Revolutionary War, after the United States became a country with its own destiny to work out, men of vision began to think about the vast land that lay between the cities of the East and the Pacific Ocean. In 1804 President Thomas Jefferson sent out a party to explore that land. Led by Meriwether Lewis and William Clark, the group was to travel to the Pacific and bring back a report on the land and the Indians and the possibility of settling those unknown regions.

The expedition took two years. Its report set imaginations aflame. Out there lay a wilderness, waiting for the skill and energy of the Yankee to turn it into a beautiful, productive land. But how to get there? No roads, no good trails, crossed the wide plains. And there were the Rockies — those shining mountains — to bar the way.

President Jefferson, a dreamer of dreams, knew that a road to the West must be built. Stirred to action by the President, Congress in 1806 passed a bill authorizing the use of federal funds for the construction of such a road. Federal money comes from all the states. The using of such funds for a project that seemed to benefit only a portion of the country was a new thing.

But the people accepted the idea, for this was to be a great road — the National Road. It would cross part of Maryland and Virginia (now West Virginia), Ohio, Indiana, and into Illinois. It was hoped that one day the road would reach St. Louis. Never, since the great days of the Romans, had any nation undertaken the construction of such a highway.

The work began, but there were problems and delays. The road plodded westward slowly, year after year. Before the dream became a reality, another had taken its place in the minds of imaginative men. These men were impatient with the slowness of coach and wagon travel. With such a vast land to be conquered, speedier travel was needed. A few men were bold enough to think that speedier travel was possible.

Stop for a moment to consider what it meant to have startling, new ideas back in the early days of our country. Today we accept such ideas with eagerness. But this was not always so. In the early nineteenth century, most people looked with suspicion on any proposal to change old ways. "What was good enough for Father is good enough for me!" was a very strong belief. Then, too, there were no words with which to express some of the dreams men were having. Thousands of words which we use today without thinking were unknown then. Such terms as "engineer," "scientist," and "inventor" were unfamiliar. And there seemed to be no place in society for men who naturally belonged in such classifications. Instead of respecting them, as we do today, their neighbors looked on them as crackpots. They were misfits in the community.

As early as 1680 Sir Isaac Newton suggested that a steam-powered vehicle such as this could be produced.

Such men, however, have been born throughout history. If their genius was great enough to overcome opposition, they helped the world take a giant step forward.

The building of the National Road was not the only result of the lure of the vast West. Even before the road was begun, some strange things were happening — things that would eventually change that wilderness into what it is today. Perhaps we should say the change started in England, though the Americans knew little about what went on over there, and this country produced its own dreamers.

Still, nearly 100 years before the American Revolution, Sir Isaac Newton suggested that steam could be used to propel a vehicle. Nothing came of this suggestion, but steam was put to use to work a piston which operated a pump.

Let us think for a moment about that piston. Men had known for centuries that if the spout of a kettle holding boiling water were stopped up, the steam would blow the stopper out. They also knew that if a bottle of boiling water were corked and then allowed to cool, the cork would be sucked down into the bottle. They knew, therefore, that water expanded as it was turned into steam and that steam contracted as it was turned into water. This push and pull, like the muscles of a man, could be used to do certain work.

Imaginative men, particularly in England, began to experiment. Sir Isaac Newton's idea seemed too farfetched to be of use. But by 1710 Thomas Newcomen had invented a workable steam pump. Some sixty years later a Scottish genius, James Watt, made some improvements in Newcomen's engine. These improvements were so valuable that Watt has been credited with giving the push that moved the whole world onto its path of invention.

In 1753 an English steam engine similar to Newcomen's was set up in the copper mines at Belleville, New Jersey. But few people were interested in the new machine. There were, however, some dreamers —crackpots to their neighbors— who were experimenting here in America with steam engines. Others were working on the idea that it would be a good thing to lay rails for the wheels of vehicles to travel on. These would enable the vehicles to move more smoothly and swiftly than they could over the rough roads. The two lines of experiment were to merge to change the face of America. A few visionaries were already looking forward to this.

One of the first successful dreamers of this wild dream was Oliver Evans. He was born in 1755 in Delaware, less than 50 miles from Belleville where that steam engine was busily pumping water from the Schuyler copper mine. But Oliver didn't know about that mine. He didn't need to. From his own mind came the idea of using a steam engine to propel a vehicle.

When he was fourteen, Oliver was apprenticed to a wagon-maker, who refused to allow the boy any time for study. The ambitious youth saved shavings from the shop, and at night he studied by the flickering light made by the burning fragments. Since he was working with wagons, he began to imagine ways of producing a *horseless* wagon. He had no books, no teachers, that could help him. None of his brothers (he was the fifth child in a family of nine) had the slightest interest in the things that kept Oliver's mind in a whirl. He had to work entirely alone, without encouragement. But work he did. By the time he was eighteen, he felt sure he could build a carriage that would run on its own power. No one was interested, and he had no way to put his idea to work.

Evans grew to manhood. He was a man of medium height, rather plump, and of a gentle, kindly disposition. He married and had a family of children. He made exciting mechanical toys for them that caused the neighborhood children to gape with envy, even though they were made by a "crazy" father. He kept a shop to provide a living for his family. But every spare minute was spent in planning and inventing. The few patent laws were unenforced, and Oliver Evans lost money on many of his practical inventions, which were used by others to their own profit.

Finding he could get nowhere with his ideas in Delaware, Evans moved to Philadelphia. There, in the largest city in the country, he hoped to find financial backing and recognition. He had only fair success in putting his inventions before the public. In 1786 he petitioned the legislatures of both Pennsylvania and Maryland for the sole right to the use of his engine in flour mills and carriages.

Pennsylvania granted this right for the flour mills but scorned any idea of steam carriages. Maryland granted both rights. The legislators observed that "whatever Evans did with steam carriages could harm no one."

Oliver Evans died in 1819 at sixty-one years of age. He never saw his dream of a horseless carriage come to reality. But he had written, "The time will come when people will travel in stages moved by steam engine, from one city to another, almost as fast as birds fly, fifteen to twenty miles an hour. . . . A carriage (steam) will set out from Washington in the morning; the passengers will breakfast at Baltimore, dine at Philadelphia and sup in New York on the same day."

To this a newspaper editor responded, "Twenty miles an hour, sir! It will set the whole world a-gadding. Grave, plodding citizens will be flying about like comets. Veracious people will turn into immeasurable liars; all their conceptions will be exaggerated by their magnificent notions of distance!"

It was to be ten years before passenger trains were put into service in America, but Oliver Evans had seen the importance of linking cities by means of steam cars.

By 1821 resistance to the new idea had so far softened that John Stevens of Hoboken, New Jersey, was granted a charter to build a railroad across that state. Two years later the Pennsylvania legislature, which had refused the petition of Oliver Evans thirty-seven years earlier, granted Stevens the right to build a railroad from Philadelphia to the Susquehannah River.

John Stevens, like Evans, was a man of original and imaginative ideas. For years he had been preaching the need for railroads. A veteran of the Revolutionary War and a member of a rich and pow-

John Stevens, one of the first American railroad enthusiasts and inventors. *Stevens Institute of Technology*

erful family, Stevens could command more attention than could Evans. He had already proposed that the United States Navy build armored ships. He had also advocated that a bridge be built across the Hudson River and a tunnel beneath it. He had urged the construction of an elevated railroad to relieve the congestion in New York City. But even he could not pry money from the states to finance his "wild" schemes.

John Stevens was obsessed with the idea that railroads were an absolute necessity if the country were to be developed as it should be. He kept pounding away at this subject until, at last, a group of businessmen founded the Pennsylvania Society for Internal Improvements. This society sent William Strickland to England to learn what was being done there. It was known that steam locomotives

The locomotive built by John Stevens in 1825 and the circular track on which it ran on his estate at Castle Point, Hoboken. *Stevens Institute of Technology*

were being built and used in that country. Strickland was to study the British system and determine whether it could be used in this country.

Meanwhile, Stevens had proved his point that a steam railroad was certainly possible. In 1825, on the level ground beside the Hudson where his great estate Castle Point lay, the seventy-six-year-old tycoon built with his own hands a steam locomotive that would actually run. In his garden John Stevens laid down a circular track for his little engine. It was a strange-looking contraption. From a four-wheeled wooden platform rose a high boiler, topped by a conical hood and a belching smokestack. Visitors to Stevens' castle were invited to take a ride, and woe to timid guests who hesitated.

16

Holding on for dear life, the valiant were whizzed around and around the track at a breathtaking six miles an hour.

It was really just a rich man's toy, yet it was actually the first steam engine to run on tracks in America. The dream had become a reality, though only in miniature.

In the same year that Stevens built his little train, Thomas Tredgold, one of the new breed of civil engineers in England, published one of the first books in the world on railroad engineering. In it was a picture of a steam-propelled locomotive drawing two loaded cars along a track. There were also sketches of the sort of track that would be needed for such a project. The book attracted little attention. People were not yet ready to accept these ideas.

The engine invented by Richard Trevithick, said to be the first locomotive in the world to do actual work.

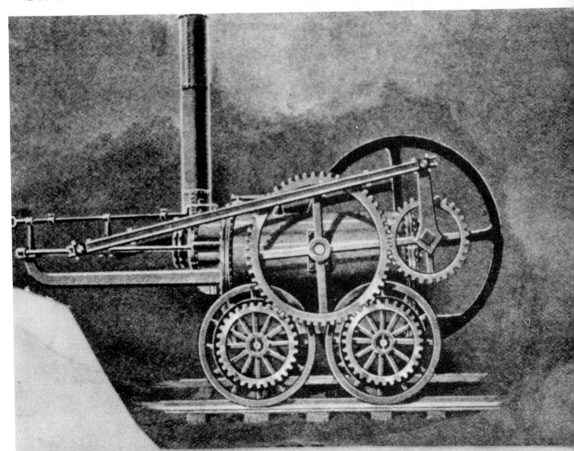

This photograph shows a model of the engine built by John Fitch. It is supposed to be the first locomotive in the world invented for railway use. *Association of American Railroads*

There were other dreamers who helped move America along the path it was destined to follow. There was the Englishman Richard Trevithick, who put a locomotive to work on a track in 1803. This has been called the first locomotive in the world to do actual work. The friends of Oliver Evans claimed that Trevithick's engine was just a copy of one Evans had invented but for the production of which he could obtain no funds.

And there was the unhappy and unfortunate American John Fitch. The engine he invented before his death in 1798 is said to have been the first engine designed for railway use. Fitch proved that a steam engine could propel a boat. His demonstration started John Stevens on his pursuit of steam railroads.

It was land transportation that had intrigued Oliver Evans. The challenge of the West had kept him searching for something to replace plodding horses and oxen. But there were still the doubters, the diehards. As one versifier put it:

> God gave man horses
> And taught him how to use them.
> Will He sit idly by
>   While men and steam abuse them?
> Such men are dangerous,
>   And I hereby accuse them
> Of trifling with Nature
>   Merely to amuse them.

2

EARLY VENTURES

John Stevens talked rail roads to everyone he thought could promote the idea. But he had little success. To most people of that time the term "rail road" simply meant two parallel wooden rails laid over an old roadbed. Between the rails a horse could walk, drawing a vehicle with its wheels on the rails. Several such rail roads were in use at mines and quarries. Others were to be constructed by cities as the idea of such travel grew.

Stevens' enthusiasm was not entirely wasted. In 1828 the Delaware and Hudson Canal Company sent Horatio Allen to England to look into the operation of steam engines and to decide whether the company should replace their horses with steam power. Allen brought back a British-made locomotive, the Stourbridge Lion. It came knocked down, and the young engineer had to put it together and get it to run. It made its trial run on August 8, 1829. It was not successful because it was too heavy for American rails. Moreover, it

For a short time horses were used to draw cars along wooden rails. This first method of railroad transportation soon gave way to the steam locomotive. *Association of American Railroads.*

Horatio Allen (1802–1890), chief engineer of the Charleston and Hamburg Railroad Company, under whose direction the Best Friend of Charleston, the West Point, and other early locomotives made their debuts. *Southern Railway System*

The double-headed locomotive South Carolina was designed by Horatio Allen to give enough power to pull this early freight train. *Southern Railway System*

was of such rigid construction it could not negotiate sharp curves. In fact, the British locomotive builders declared no engines could be constructed to make sharp curves. It was up to the Americans themselves to solve the problem.

Young Allen was equal to the challenge. He left the Delaware and Hudson Canal Company and went to work for the newly chartered Charleston and Hamburg Railroad Company at Charleston, South Carolina. There he designed the Best Friend of Charleston, the locomotive which was to draw the first regularly scheduled passenger trains and the first mail carried by rail.

On Christmas morning, 1830, the Best Friend took its initial trip over a six-mile-long track. It pulled a brigade (train) of cars filled with cheering, exultant passengers. This short first trip was a success from every point of view. It was followed by other demonstration runs, and regular schedules began with a bang in January, 1831.

And a bang it was! A small field gun was placed in one of the carriages and was fired every little while as the train sped along at 21 miles an hour. Behind the puffing locomotive, more than 200 businessmen and their families cheered and sang and dug cinders from their eyes.

Six months later the first railroad explosion occurred — another first for the Charleston and Hamburg line. A Negro workman was helping turn the engine around on the revolving platform at the end of the line. The sound of the escaping steam bothered him. To stop the noise, he sat down on the valve. The noise stopped all right, but the steam was not so obedient. It exploded with a roar. Bits of iron pipe were sent hurtling through the air. The workman was so seriously injured that he later died.

The locomotive West Point with the barrier car devised by Horatio Allen. Bales of cotton piled on a flatcar were to protect passengers from a possible explosion of the steam boiler. *Southern Railway System*

Even before Horatio Allen had been sent to England, Maryland had granted a charter to the Baltimore and Ohio Railroad Company. This is the oldest extant railroad charter in America. The line was to have a long and distinguished history.

One of the promoters of this company was Peter Cooper, a New York businessman. Cooper was a thin-faced, beak-nosed man, with a fringe of beard decorating his chin. He was a very rich merchant, manufacturer, and inventor, whose memory has been perpetuated in the names of Cooperstown, New York, and Peter Cooper Village and Cooper Union in New York City. In front of the Cooper Union building is a statue of the founder.

Cooper owned land in Maryland that would be more valuable, he thought, if a railroad could be built to the Ohio River to compete with the Erie Canal. Completed in 1825, this canal, like the National

Road, was an attempt to bring the interior of the country into closer communication with the cities of the East. The canal had proved very successful. Buffalo and New York City, its terminals, were booming. Peter Cooper thought that a steam railroad could do for Baltimore what the Erie Canal had done for New York City.

Work began on July 4, 1828, just outside Baltimore. The groundbreaking celebration was a merry one — the first of scores of jollifications that accompanied the building of American railroads. All the great and powerful businessmen of the city were on hand. Aged Charles Carroll, the only surviving signer of the Declaration of Independence, lifted the first shovelful of dirt. In his speech he declared that this was one of the greatest moments of his life, second only to his signing that great document. "And maybe not even second to that!" he added.

At a ceremony commemorating the laying of the first stone of the Baltimore and Ohio Railroad, citizens of Baltimore reenact that historic event. Holding the shovel is one who represented the aged Charles Carroll, the last surviving signer of the Declaration of Independence. *Baltimore and Ohio Railroad*

A special song was composed for this historic event. The crowd shouted, rather than sang:

> There's a road to be made
> With a pick and a spade,
> 'Tis to reach to the Ohio
> For the benefit of trade;
> There are mountains to be level'd,
> And valleys to be filled;
> There are rocks to be blown out,
> And bridges too, to build.
>
> And we're all hopping, skipping, jumping,
> And we're all crazy here in Baltimore.

The work went very slowly. When 13 miles of track had been laid to Ellicott's Mills at a tremendous expense, the company was about ready to give up. The chief problem was caused by the curves of the track. The heavy, British-built engines could not follow such sharp curves and ran off the track whenever they came to one. Yet curves were necessary in this terrain. It looked hopeless. Peter Cooper did not want to lose all the money he had invested in the company. He said he would manufacture an engine that could take the curves. His iron mines and iron foundries would have his locomotive ready before the year was out.

Peter Cooper had been called the honest man. In this case he proved to be as good as his word. He put together a strange little contraption which he named the Tom Thumb. It was a makeshift affair, constructed of old wheels and a wooden platform, with a boiler six feet high. Gun barrels were used for pipes because no iron pipes were made in America at that time.

In August, 1830, the Tom Thumb sat on the tracks near Baltimore, ready for a trial run to Ellicott's Mills. Six men crowded onto the shaky platform, and twenty more piled onto the little car attached to the locomotive. Away they went! They covered the 13 miles in a little more than an hour and returned in fifteen minutes' less time. The watching crowds cheered, guns were fired, and bands played. The Tom Thumb was a success.

The canalboat and stagecoach owners had not been asleep. They saw what was happening and knew that the newfangled transportation was a real threat to their business. If they could only prove that the railroad with its steam locomotives was more dangerous and slower than horse-powered coaches, they could perhaps stave off this threat. Stockton and Stokes, the leading stagecoach company of Baltimore, challenged the Tom Thumb to a race with a horse-drawn car. Two tracks had been laid to Ellicott's Mills. The Tom Thumb was ready on one; the powerful stagecoach horse, hitched to a car, stood pawing the ground on the other. Both the locomotive and the horse were pulling cars loaded with passengers.

The word "Go!" was shouted, and the big gray horse leaped ahead. The Tom Thumb, however, was having a bit of trouble getting up steam. The passengers on both cars shouted jeers and catcalls at their competitors. Finally, the little engine began to move, the engineer leaning forward to help it along, the fireman piling on wood. Faster and faster went the Tom Thumb, catching up with and passing the wagon.

The driver whipped up his horse, shouting commands, and the big animal responded nobly, and for a while he kept even with the

This painting by H. D. Stitt represents the race between the Tom Thumb and the stage-coach horse. The subject has been painted many times. *Baltimore and Ohio Railroad*

engine. Then he began to slow down. The Tom Thumb pulled ahead while the railroad passengers jeered in triumph. But their jubilation was premature. Something went wrong, and the little locomotive slackened speed. Peter Cooper, who was, of course, running the engine in this historic race, tried to repair the damage but could not. Meanwhile, the horse had regained his breath, and he galloped ahead and won the race.

It was a sad blow for those who advocated steam rather than horsepower. The disappointment did not last long. Other steam locomotives were proving their worth in various sections of the East, and one defeat could not stop their progress.

One of these successful steam engines was the De Witt Clinton, which took a trainload of excited passengers from Albany to Schenectady on August 9, 1831. A reporter and silhouette artist named

William H. Brown happened to be one of those passengers. His description of the ride and the silhouette he made of the train have been preserved. They give a vivid eyewitness account of the journey that cannot be improved on. A part of his article will tell the story:

It [the locomotive] was a small affair, only ten or twelve feet long, with large wheels, a high smokestack and a central dome. At the rear was an open platform on which the engineer could stand to operate the train. Behind this was a small flat car carrying wood and water for the engine. A leather hose ran from the water barrels to the engine. Three passenger cars, resembling stage coaches, had seats for six people, with room for a few others at the ends. Interest in this test run was so great that the company added five

This locomotive, the Atlantic, was put into operation on the Baltimore and Ohio in the summer of 1832. It is drawing a small train of double-deck Imlay coaches. It shows that the B&O did not give up the idea of steam after the Tom Thumb lost its race. *Baltimore and Ohio Railroad*

The De Witt Clinton, the third locomotive built in America, took excursionists from Albany to Schenectady and back on August 9, 1831. This view is of one of its later trips. *New York Central System*

or six flat cars behind the coaches. These had long benches to accommodate the extra people who insisted on taking the ride. This was the first steam train ever assembled in New York state, and a huge crowd gathered to observe its performance.

When all the cars were filled, the "Captain" collected the tickets; then he took his place on a little seat on the water and fuel car, blew a blast on his tin horn, and the train started. But not all at once! The cars were joined together by an iron chain some three feet long. As the engine leaped forward, the "Captain" was jerked nearly out of his seat. A moment later, the first car started with a jerk that snapped the passengers backward into a heap. A moment later, the same thing happened in the second coach, and then, one by one, in each of the following cars. But when all were in motion, the people picked themselves up, resumed their seats and began to enjoy the ride.

But not for long! The smokestack now began belching forth great clouds of smoke lighted by blazing sparks from the wood-burning engine. The passengers in the three coaches were somewhat protected by the roof of their car, but those on the flat cars behind found themselves in danger of being burnt alive. Some had umbrellas with them — for protection against the August sun. They raised these now to protect them from the sparks. But alas! the sparks soon set the umbrellas ablaze, and the flaming objects had to be tossed overboard, where they started fires in the dry grass beside the roadbed.

Several of the women passengers found their light summer dresses had caught fire, but their neighbors came to their rescue, beating out the small flames with hands and hats and hastily jerked off coats.

Thus they moved along till they came to the place where the water barrels were to be refilled. The engineer applied his brakes and the locomotive stopped with a jerk. The water-and-wood car banged into its rear end with a crash, and each coach, being attached by the loose chain, smashed into the one ahead. This time the passengers were again piled into heaps, as at starting, only they were all crushed in the front, instead of the rear end.

When they regained their feet, the passengers went to work to correct the troubles that had beset them. They put out all the little fires that still smouldered on their clothing.

Then they took axes, carried on the train to use in replenishing the wood for the engine, and cut down a neighboring fence. They chopped the rails into lengths which they could wedge between the cars to make the train a firm unit, and so prevent the jerks at starting and stopping.

The train continued its journey and was declared an unqualified success. The Albany newspaper mentioned that the run had been made. It said, "The engine performed the entire route (17 miles) in less than an hour, including stoppages, and at a part of the road the speed was at the rate of thirty miles an hour."

Old Ironsides was built by Matthias Baldwin and made its trial run on November 23, 1832, on the Philadelphia, Germantown and Norristown Railroad. *Reading Company*

The public was becoming convinced of the value of steam loco-motives and railroads. The converted were filled with a new enthu-siasm and excitement that amounted almost to a near-frenzy. This was the onset of the railroad fever that was to grip the country for 100 years. It became so prevalent that one visitor observed, "Amer-icans love their railroads with a passion."

Perhaps they did. Perhaps they only felt, rather than understood, that here was the answer to the problem of building a great, unified nation that would stretch from sea to sea. The slow prairie schooners were to serve for some 40 more years. But the task was too great for the lumbering wagons. Only the steam railroad could do the job ahead.

3

YANKEE INGENUITY GOES TO WORK

The report by William Brown on the Albany-Schenectady trip revealed the most obvious defects of the first trains. These were the manner in which the cars were joined together, or coupled, as railway jargon called it; the danger of sparks from the smokestack; the open cab, on which the engineer rode unprotected; and the problem of wood and water.

These were problems which American engineers had to solve for themselves. It was no use looking to England. The British locomotives had already proved useless on American roads. But Yankee ingenuity could solve these problems, as it had solved one by using fence rails to make the Schenectady-bound train a rigid unit to avoid the jerks that piled the passengers in heaps.

We already know that Horatio Allen went to England and brought back the Stourbridge Lion. When it proved unable to negotiate American curves, Allen began to design his own locomotives.

Another young American engineer, Isaac Dripps, did the same thing. He brought over from England the John Bull for the Camden and Amboy Railroad of New Jersey. Dripps was in charge of putting the engine together, and in doing so, he learned a great deal. He did the job so well that this English locomotive saw more than 100 years of service and may now be seen in the Smithsonian Institution in Washington, D.C. But Dripps was not content with merely assembling knocked-down engines. He wanted to design locomotives that would have features no British engine had. As he worked, he introduced devices that developed into the standard American engine. Other Yankee designers were also putting their skill and ability to the task of perfecting the steam locomotive for railroad use.

That ride to Schenectady had proved that the entire train of separate cars must move as a unit. Somehow the cars had to be joined together so they would not bump into each other at starting and stopping. For a time iron bars were used between the cars. But these sometimes broke, especially if the cars were heavily loaded. Finally, the link and pin coupler was invented.

To couple cars, an iron link on the front of one car was inserted into a socket on the rear of another and held in place by an iron pin. This was a very dangerous maneuver for the trainman, because he had to stand between the two cars to guide the link into the socket. Then he had to insert the pin by hand. If one or both of the cars happened to be jolted, the workman might easily lose a finger or a whole hand. Often he was crushed between the cars and killed. Still, the link and pin coupler was used until after the Civil War.

In 1868 Eli Hamilton Janney patented an automatic coupler, which worked whenever the cars came together. No manual operation was needed. Janney made various improvements on his original design, and in several tests it was proved to be an excellent device. It was not, however, adopted immediately. In 1876 the Pennsylvania Railroad installed it on all its cars, but the automatic coupler did not entirely replace the link and pin until the 1890's.

The flying sparks from the wood-burning engines were to prove a danger for many years. Several attempts were made to eliminate the trouble. One of the strangest inventions was a smokestack that ran back the entire length of the train. The sparks from such a smokestack could not injure the passengers, but this did not keep them from setting fires along the route. Finally, a screen was placed over the top of the smokestack. This helped, but sparks still managed to get through the mesh. For years, every railroad company employed a great many trackwalkers to make sure that every little flame was extinguished.

Since most of the early bridges were made of wood, they were particularly likely to be set on fire by the sparks. To avoid this danger, a permanent watchman was engaged at every bridge. He had several hogsheads of water handy with which to douse the sparks before they could do any damage.

Another problem of the wood-burning engine was the impossibility of carrying enough fuel for a long run. When the initial load had been consumed, the train crew — and often the passengers — would alight to gather more. Axes were carried for this wooding up, and no farmer's orchard or fence was safe from the eager travelers.

Even after coal displaced wood as fuel on most trains, smoke and cinders bothered the passengers. The first successful use of coal was in 1855, when the Daniel Webster proved that this fuel was only half as expensive and twice as effective as wood. In spite of this, coal was not generally used until some twenty years later. Today the few old wood burners have an aura of romance lacked by engines that use other fuel — coal or oil or electricity.

The first trains had scant provision for the engineer. He stood on an open platform at the rear of the engine. There he was bombarded by sparks and soot from the engine, pelted by snow and rain, whipped by the wind. It was 1842 before a covered cab was added by some lines and many years later before this feature was adopted by all lines.

William Brown reported of the famous Albany-Schenectady trip that the "Captain blew a blast on his tin horn and the train started." This was a holdover from the canalboats that had used a horn to announce arrivals and departures. The first locomotives had no whistles. Sometimes, when the engineer wished to attract the attention of the captain (today's conductor), he would raise the valve on the dome, either with his hand or with a stick. This would let the steam escape with a loud hiss. Although this was the usual practice, it was years before this steam was used to activate a whistle.

In 1836 the first locomotives known to have been equipped with whistles were built at Lowell, Massachusetts. It is interesting that this was the achievement of a man named Whistler — George Washington Whistler. The general public did not immediately take to the new noise. It was described as a "shrill, wild unearthly sound something like drawing a saw flat across a bar of iron." Another citizen said the trains gave "an awful notice" of their approach.

Later, as rails stretched across the lonely prairies and isolated villages, the train whistle came to be waited for and loved. It spoke of far places, of romance and mystery. The poet Emily Dickinson used to lie in the woods to watch the train sweep by. She wrote that she loved "to hear it lap the miles and lick the valleys up." To others the whistle had a mournful sound. An old song says, "Lord, I hate to hear that mournful whistle blow!"

There were certain definite signals that all trains used: two long blasts for starting; one long, tremulous cry when approaching a station; and the mournful *whooooo, whooooo, whooooo!* at grade crossings. Some engineers put their own personality into their signaling. Casey Jones was one of these:

> The switchman knew by the engine's moans
> That the man at the throttle was Casey Jones.

And there was the fictional Zack, the Mormon engineer:

> When he'd whistle, "Whooo — Whooo!"
> Mama'd understand
> That Zack was headed homeward
> On the Denver and Rio Grande.

At first no thought was given to overcoming the slickness of the rails caused by snow or ice. Then, in 1836, Pennsylvania suffered from a plague of grasshoppers. The insects were so thick on the tracks that when the wheels crushed them, the mess made the wheels spin. The trains could not go. The railroad companies tried sending men ahead to sweep the tracks, but the grasshoppers swarmed down as soon as the men had passed. Scrapers were tried, but they slowed the trains too much. Brooms were fastened to the front of the engine, but they wore out too fast. Finally, someone had the idea of placing a sandbox on the front of the engine. The sand automatically poured down from the box onto the track. This proved effective against the grasshoppers and was later used on icy rails. For a long time the sandbox was standard equipment on American locomotives.

Grasshoppers plagued the railroads for years, but they were not the only critters to cause trouble. Horses, cows, pigs, and sheep had not learned that a railroad right-of-way was a poor place to loiter. All through the countryside, these animals were a danger to themselves and to the trains. Isaac Dripps put his mind to the problem and produced the first cowcatcher.

This was an apt name for the device. It consisted of several long, pointed iron bars that extended some three feet in front of the engine, a few inches above the rails. The pointed bars were expected to impale any animal straying along the track, and to keep it from falling in front of the engine and throwing the train off the rails. It worked

This engine, the Stevens, was built in 1850 for the Camden and Amboy Railroad. It had six truck wheels and two large driving wheels, a huge smokestack, an early cowcatcher, and no headlight. *Pennsylvania Railroad*

This shows the first attempt at lighting the track ahead of the engine. Worked out by Horatio Allen, it was never very widely used. *Southern Railway*

too perfectly. The first victim was a huge bull, which was caught so tightly by the prongs that it required great effort to pry him loose. So this first cowcatcher had to be discarded and a less deadly one designed. The cowcatcher finally became a series of slanting iron rods of varying lengths, rimmed by a heavy bar. This formed a sort of triangular pusher that could remove an animal without killing it. Or so it was hoped.

For a time no headlight was needed because there was no travel at night. As traffic increased and night runs became necessary, experiments were made in ways of lighting up the track so the engineer could see whether there was any obstruction ahead of him.

When Horatio Allen was in charge of the Charleston and Hamburg line, he built a small flatcar, put on it a bed of sand, and on the sand lighted a fire of pine logs. This car was placed in front of the engine and provided light that was better than nothing. But the device was not generally accepted by other railroads. Some lines tried candles, protected by glass. Even when tin reflectors were put behind the candles, they gave little light. Later, lamps were used — at first they burned whale oil. Then, after oil was discovered in Pennsylvania, kerosene lamps were tried. When electric lamps proved practical, they were installed on the locomotives. Today the sealed beam headlight throws a powerful beam of light that illuminates the track almost as clearly as the sun's rays.

On the earliest trains there was no way for the engineer to communicate with the captain or for the captain to let the engineer know if some emergency arose. After Captain Ayers of the Erie Railroad rigged up a cord and a stick of wood with which to attract the engineer's attention, other devices were tried. These resulted in the cord and bell system still in use. But today the conductor merely presses a button that rings the emergency bell.

All this time engineers were experimenting to find the best type and number of wheels to use on their engines. They tried four small wheels in front and two large ones behind; six small wheels followed by two large ones; eight medium-size wheels; and many other arrangements. Finally, the standard became four small wheels on the rotatable truck, at the front end, with four large driving wheels behind. This arrangement became known as the American type and was generally used on all railroads in the country.

The first brakes were similar to those used on stagecoaches. A foot-operated lever pushed a block of wood against the wheels to slow them down. On one Pennsylvania railroad an even more primitive method was used to stop the train. As the engineer approached a station, he let the steam escape from the valve with a loud hiss. This was a signal to the roustabouts employed to rush out, grab the engine with their hands, and lean back, digging their heels into the ground. The station agent would then thrust a stout stick between the spokes of one of the engine's wheels. With strong-armed fellows using all their strength, the train could be stopped within a few yards.

It was not until after the Civil War that adequate brakes were installed. In 1869 George Westinghouse, just twenty-two years old, patented his air brake. Few railroads put this safety feature on their trains until some twenty-four years later, when the Railroad Safety Appliance Act was passed by Congress and signed into law by President Benjamin Harrison. That day, March 2, 1893, has been called the greatest day in railroad history. The law required that air brakes and automatic coupling be installed on all trains, both passenger and freight. Accidents to railroad employees dropped to less than half what they had been before.

A number of men who were devoting their lives to perfecting the steam locomotive are remembered for their work. We have already mentioned Horatio Allen and Isaac Dripps. John B. Jervis built the first rotatable truck — a front end that was connected to the rear in such a way that it could swivel. This allowed the engine to

George Westinghouse, whose air brake did much to lessen accidents on the railroads of America. *Association of American Railroads*

42

The Experiment, designed by John B. Jervis, early railway engineering genius, was in its day the fastest locomotive in the world. It was a familiar sight on the Mohawk and Hudson Railroad, the first railroad in the state of New York and the original unit of the New York Central System. *New York Central System*

negotiate sharp curves. Henry Campbell was the man who developed and patented the American type of engine. Ross Winans, designing for the Baltimore and Ohio, made many improvements on the engines used by his company.

Winans' locomotives were among the most beautiful in the country. They were painted in bright, clear colors, with red and blue, green and yellow predominating. In fact, all the locomotives of the early period were gaily painted, as were the tenders. These were open cars attached to the locomotive. They carried the fuel for the engine. Often on their flat sides were painted scenes of the route traveled, the name of the railroad in fancy scrolls, or the portrait of some famous man.

And, of course, all locomotives were given romantic names: the Best Friend of Charleston, the Highland Light, the Accommodation, the De Witt Clinton, the President, the Tiger. As William

The first locomotive with eight wheels was designed by H. R. Campbell in 1836. *Association of American Railroads*

This is a typical locomotive built by the Baldwin Company of Philadelphia. Matthias Baldwin was a jewelry maker, who became a leading locomotive builder. His first engines were miniatures, made to run on a small track in a museum. *Baldwin Locomotive Works*

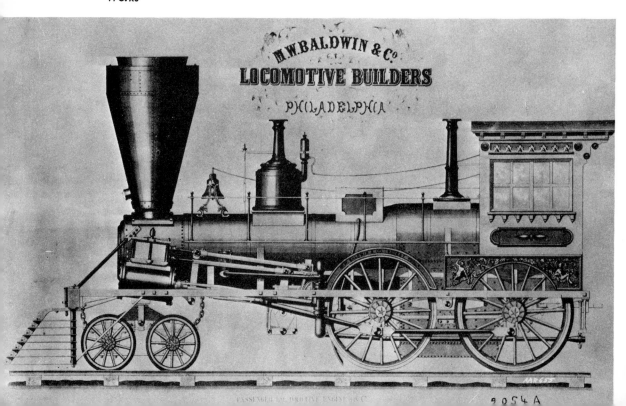

This locomotive, designed by Ross Winans in 1848, was called a camel because the cab was on top of the boiler, not behind it. *Association of American Railroads*

Mason, one of the great artists in locomotive designing, said, these early builders felt that an engine should look "somewhat better than a cookstove on wheels." Yankee inventiveness was producing the finest railroad engines in the world.

The locomotive was not the only part of the train that was being improved. A great deal of attention was being paid to the passenger cars. Complaints from passengers, the competition between companies, and the editorials in newspapers and magazines — all were influential in bringing about changes. For many years Sarah J. Hale was editor of *Godey's Lady's Book*, one of the widest-read magazines in the country. Mrs. Hale was alert to the problems of the day and tried to keep her readers informed of what was going on. To learn firsthand what the newfangled transportation offered to women travelers, she sent an alert young lady, Eliza Leslie, from New York to Niagara Falls. Miss Leslie was to observe and report on everything

The Tiger was a beautifully decorated locomotive, built for fast passenger service in 1856. It had a cowcatcher, a lamp headlight, a covered cab, and eight wheels. Its smokestack was streamlined in comparison with others, and it carried a flag to wave boldly as the train sped along. It was, in fact, one of the finest locomotives of the day. *Association of American Railroads*

she saw and experienced. Her stories in the *Lady's Book* gave women for the first time an accurate picture of railroad travel, and Mrs. Hale's comments and editorials helped bring about many improvements in the accommodations for passengers.

The style of the passenger coaches was already different from the early styles that copied the stagecoach. They had become long, narrow cars, the shape of which has not changed greatly to the present time. At first the seats were long wooden benches along the length of the car. Then the arrangement was changed to two rows of seats, with a center aisle between them. This arrangement, too, has not been greatly changed. Gradually the uncomfortable, hard wooden seats were upholstered, springs were added, reclining backs replaced the straight upright backs, and footrests were provided. It took many years, but a fairly comfortable seat was the final result.

For a while candles, then gas and kerosene lamps, were used to light the cars at night. A large wood-burning stove at one end of the car warmed it in winter. Neither light nor heat was very satisfactory. Passengers sitting right under a lamp could see dimly; the rest were in deep shadow. Those close to the stove were too hot; those a short distance away had no warmth at all. And both lamps and stoves were very dangerous. A wreck of any kind, even an otherwise harmless derailment, would upset them, starting fires that were far more disastrous than the original wreck. After electric lights and steam heat were introduced, this danger was eliminated.

The observant Miss Leslie had reported that there was no drinking water in the cars. This was particularly unfortunate, Mrs. Hale declared in an editorial, for women traveling with children. The work of the two women stimulated complaints from passengers, but eleven years later this defect had not been remedied. In 1856 the publisher himself, Louis Antoine Godey, took a month's holiday to travel "abroad," from Philadelphia to St. Paul. It was summertime, and the portly Godey suffered from the heat. What annoyed the publisher most was the lack of drinking water. "It would be simple to have a tank of drinking water in each car," he wrote. He went on to ask, "And why not sell ham sandwiches at the stations?"

Both suggestions were acted on some years later. The tank of water had a tin drinking cup attached to it by a chain — to prevent its being carried off. All passengers drank from the same cup. On one trip a woman let her dog have a drink. When the men in the car protested, the lady declared that her dog's tongue was far cleaner than the men's beards and mustaches which were draggled into the cup when the men took a drink. The tin cup and chain lasted well into the twentieth century, when today's paper cups replaced them.

About 1837 the line from Philadelphia to Norristown, Pennsylvania, made a startling innovation. A tiny room was set apart at each end of the long car. One was for women passengers who wished to refresh themselves; the other was for men. This was the first time that any provision, other than benches, had ever been made for the comfort of the traveler.

As for night travel — the passengers just sprawled on the hard wooden seats. Men could remove their shoes and ties and rest their feet on the back of the seat ahead. But the modesty of the time prevented women from removing anything but their bonnets. Then, in 1837, another Pennsylvania line designed a car that offered slightly better accommodations. The seats along one side of the center aisle could be changed into a row of bunks. Above them, wooden shelves

Scene in an early sleeping car. Only men passengers were permitted. *New York Central System*

could be let down to form two upper tiers. There were no mattresses, pillows, sheets, or blankets, and passengers paid fifty to seventy-five cents for the privilege of stretching out on the bare wood. By 1858 George Pullman's sleeping cars were being tried out.

As Godey had noted, there was no help for the hungry passenger. At certain stations, passengers were permitted to hurry away to the nearest hotel to gulp down a hasty meal. Some always loitered, and the train was delayed. Finally, Godey's suggestion was not only acted on, but improved. Sandwiches, candy, cigars, and newspapers were sold right in the cars. Later, dining cars were added.

Thus, in the twenty years between 1830 and 1850, the distinctive world of the American railroad emerged. Many improvements were brought about through complaints of passengers. Others were due to the artistic ability of the builders. By 1850 the American locomotive was pulling American-designed passenger and freight cars. The locomotives were the best in the world and were being sold to European countries. The passenger cars were already showing features designed for the comfort and convenience of passengers. Even steel springs had been added to prevent the "shaking and jogging that is injurious to the health." Such attention to the well-being of travelers was new and strange. But in the years ahead the traveler was to be the important factor in building America, and the railroads were to carry him.

4

A JOB TO BE DONE

One of the biggest tasks facing the young Republic was to make that vast stretch of land from the Atlantic to the Pacific one unified nation. By the Louisiana Purchase in 1803, the United States had bought from France nearly 1,000,000 square miles of land west of the Mississippi River. This was most of the territory between the river and the Rocky Mountains. In 1848, by treaty with Mexico, the southwest area from the Rockies to the Pacific was obtained. The land claimed by the United States through discovery, occupation, and treaty was a great region waiting to be made a vital part of the growing nation.

While engineers and designers were improving the trains, the railroad companies were turning their attention more directly to the problem of building up the interior. At the same time they would be promoting their own development and the growth of the Eastern cities where these companies originated.

A timetable issued in the late 1850's by the Orange and Alexandria Railroad. *Southern Railway System*

The Baltimore and Ohio Railroad, as we have seen, was chartered with this very purpose in view. For a while after the race between the coach horse and the Tom Thumb, the use of steam engines was abandoned. But not for long. Faster than the horses could draw the trains of cars, the rails were being laid westward. Travelers and goods were being carried back and forth between the ends of the rails and Baltimore. Twenty-six passengers had ridden behind the Tom Thumb on that historic race. Five years later, with only 60 miles of track laid, the line carried 97,786 passengers during the year. In 1852 the Baltimore and Ohio rails reached Wheeling, Virginia (now in West Virginia).

Sturdy locomotives designed by William Mason pulled freight and passenger cars across Maryland and Virginia to tap the rich

51

resources of the country and to carry settlers to the fast-growing settlements. On its own tracks, or through connections with other lines, some of which it leased, the Baltimore and Ohio reached St. Louis by 1857 and Chicago by 1874.

Farther north, in New York State, the great "Work of the Age" was outracing its competitors. This was the New York and Erie Railroad. It had been dreamed up by a group of businessmen who favored steam locomotives over steamboats, railroads over canals. When the Erie Canal had first been proposed, John Stevens had advocated a railroad instead of the canal, but many people thought such a project was not practical.

After the canal was opened, William C. Redfield published a pamphlet called the *Geographical Route of a Great Railway*. It outlined a route from the navigable waters of New York State to the Great Lakes and the Mississippi River. A map showed exactly where the rails could be laid to avoid any impossible barrier. This pamphlet was to be a guideline for the railroad which was later built.

In August, 1833, the New York and Erie Railroad Company was organized, and work began. Then a disastrous fire in New York City, a financial panic, fights among the workmen, riots, and various other troubles delayed progress of the rails. Farmers who could not see any advantage in having the Iron Horse snorting along the country roads piled obstructions on the tracks. The Indians along the route did anything they could to stop the menace. Money ran out, and there were delays while more was being found. There were changes in designs and materials. The gauge — or distance between rails — was altered several times. This meant re-laying some portions of track. Finally, the original six-foot gauge was abandoned, and a four-foot, eight-and-a-half-inch gauge was adopted. The rails advanced.

At last the great project was completed. In May, 1851, the first train traveled from Pierpont on the Hudson to Dunkirk on Lake Erie. It carried 280 very distinguished passengers, including President Millard Fillmore and Daniel Webster. Webster sat in a rocking chair firmly fastened to the bed of a flatcar so he could view all the scenic wonders of the route.

As the train came to each little town, it was greeted by crowds of cheering people. Flags waved, bunting flapped in the breeze, bands played, and church bells peeled out the glad news that the railroad had arrived. Banners all along the way proclaimed a welcome to the "Work of the Age." At Dunkirk it was greeted by a twenty-one-gun salute from the USS *Michigan* standing in the harbor.

> 'Tis the work of the Age,
>   Gigantic and stupendous;
> 'Twill build up the country
>   It's value is tremendous —
> So cheer, boys, cheer
> For the great Erie Railroad!

In spite of all the rejoicing, the Erie had bad luck for most of its life. During the first two months there were sixteen serious accidents. One of these involved the great wooden trestle that had been built over the Genesee River. It was a huge, matchstick affair that had taken two years to build and had cost $175,000. It swayed and groaned and threatened to fall every time a train of cars passed over it. In 1852 flying sparks turned it into a roaring bonfire that could be seen for 40 miles.

Other accidents followed fast, but they were not the worst disasters suffered by this railroad. It was only a few years old when a rascal named Daniel Drew acquired a large block of stock by shady dealings. He became treasurer of the company. With two other scoundrel friends, James Fisk and Jay Gould, he began to build his own and his friends' fortunes by various crooked deals. Many who put up money to help the railroad lost their investments.

But in spite of its troubles, the Erie Railroad won a place in history. The term "Work of the Age" was not a great exaggeration. When the line was completed, it was 450 miles long — the longest railroad in the United States. It curved across the lower part of New York State and did much to build up that region.

It was after the railroad came that Binghamton became the country's second-largest tobacco-manufacturing city. Then shoe manufacturing brought thousands of immigrants to settle there. Factories, tanneries, and rubber mills shot up. Owego, Elmira, Corning, and other cities, some more than 100 years old, were suddenly filled with new life and energy. The railroads brought in raw materials and workers and carried away the finished products.

Other sections of the country, seeing what a railroad could do, were hastening to build lines. Philadelphia had long been the largest city and the most important seaport in the country. Businessmen in that city saw their prestige threatened by booming New York State. They knew that something had to be done for Pennsylvania.

At first they considered building a canal-and-river system westward across the state to Pittsburgh and the Ohio River. This idea was discarded because the Allegheny Mountains, rising to a height of more than 2,000 feet, made such a project impracticable. It seemed that the answer lay in a railroad if the cars could somehow be hoisted over this mountain barrier.

A few miles west of Philadelphia was a hill 187 feet high. Engineers of the Pennsylvania Railroad set to work to find a way to get a train over this hill. If this could be done, they would tackle the greater obstacle of the Alleghenies. Up the side of the hill they constructed an inclined plane from the foot to the top. Tracks were laid on this plane; pulleys and ropes were installed at the top. It was found necessary to use a rope nine inches in diameter, costing $2,800, to pull a train of cars to the top of the hill. But the cars reached the top without mishap.

Now the engineers were ready to tackle the mountain. In the 36½ miles between Hollidaysburg and Johnstown loomed this 2,300-foot barrier. The State of Pennsylvania owned the railroad. It furnished the money to construct a series of inclined planes and to purchase the machinery for hoisting the cars to the top and lowering them on the other side, at Johnstown. There the traveler could take a canalboat to Pittsburgh. In 1834 the journey from Philadelphia to Pittsburgh by horse-drawn cars, steam railroad, canalboats, and riverboats could be made in four days. In 1852, when the Pennsylvania Railroad Company had completed a line all the way to Pittsburgh, the canalboats were doomed and gradually disappeared as a major means of transportation across the state.

Here again the railroad worked miracles. Since the early 1800's Johnstown had been sending iron ore to the mills at Pittsburgh. With the discovery of bituminous coal and the arrival of the railroad, the city became a steel center in its own right. The population of Hollidaysburg leaped from 72 to 1,896 as the railroad was built across the state. Railroads helped in the industrial development of the state's capital, Harrisburg. Altoona did not begin to develop as an industrial center until after Archibald Wright sold 35 acres of land to the Pennsylvania Railroad Company for a depot, offices, and shops. Again, the railroad had turned a sleepy agricultural region into a busy industrial area that would benefit the entire country.

There was another great line penetrating the interior, developing resources, and building cities as it went. This was the New York Central, which built and bought lines to form a continuous route from Albany to Buffalo.

In Albany, New York, lived a shrewd nail maker named Erastus Corning. Corning had made a good deal of money selling land to the Erie Railroad, and a town not far from Elmira had been named for him. Now he began to think that the lower part of the state should not have all the business provided by a railroad. A line from Albany to Buffalo ought to be a good thing.

He looked over the land and found that there were nearly a dozen short lines connecting towns in that area. Very quietly, he bought up ten of these lines. When the gaps between them were bridged by new tracks, Corning had the railroad he wanted. He named it the New York Central Railroad, and it was completed on August 1, 1853. It was 542 miles long, nearly 100 miles longer than its rival, the Erie. Corning made many improvements on his lines. He had better tracks put down, he bought new, powerful locomotives, and he installed conveniences for the passengers. The system flourished.

Now the officers of the company decided they ought to have a line connecting Albany with New York City. But this time they ran into difficulty.

One of the great geniuses of the railroad age was Cornelius Vanderbilt of New York City. Vanderbilt was a great seaman and liked to be called the Commodore. He was also very clever with money. He was watching the New York Central, and he decided it would soon want to come on to New York City. But the old Commodore, who was in his seventies, wanted the New York Central. He went to work, and by clever, somewhat shady, and very complicated manipulations, he managed to purchase that entire system. He had already bought up a small, unprofitable line from Albany to New York, so now Commodore Vanderbilt owned a line from New York City to Buffalo.

The old Commodore did not plan to stop here. He wanted to go on to Chicago, which was beginning to look as if it would be the great railway center of the country. With the money he was making by his shrewd deals, he purchased the Lake Shore and Michigan Railroad, which ran from Buffalo to Chicago. And he bought other lines he thought would further his scheme of a great network of railroads with headquarters in New York City. His railroads were to build not only the country but also his personal fortune. When he died in 1880 at the age of eighty-six, he left $75,000,000, the largest personal fortune made up to that time in the United States.

During the years that the Baltimore and Ohio, the Erie, the Pennsylvania, and the New York Central railroads were being built, tracks were being laid in other states and regions to connect important cities. In the twenty-five years from 1830 to 1855, Louisiana,

Delaware, New Jersey, South Carolina, Virginia, Alabama, Kentucky, Massachusetts, Rhode Island, Ohio, Michigan, Maine, Florida, Mississippi, Georgia, Illinois, Indiana, New Hampshire, Connecticut, Tennessee, Vermont, and Wisconsin all were benefiting from railroads. In 1851 the first international railway link on the North American continent joined Laprairie, Quebec, to Rouses Point, New York. A year later the Pacific drew the first train west of the Mississippi. It made a run of five miles from St. Louis to Cheltenham (now included in St. Louis), Missouri.

America had swung into the railroad age, and many parts of the country were enjoying the benefits of the steam trains.

5

PROBLEMS ARE SOLVED

The railroad line from Baltimore to Ellicott's Mills, over which the Tom Thumb raced, was 13 miles long. The distance from Albany to Schenectady was 17 miles. These seemed marvels of distance for a train to travel. Yet in a few years the New York Central had cars running over 542 miles of track.

As roads grew longer and equipment more convenient and expensive, some problems that had previously not been too bothersome now had to be met and solved. One of the most important was: Who should own the railroads?

When Ohio became a state back in 1802, Congress passed a bill that gave the state certain federal lands which were to be sold, and part of the money was to be used for building roads within the state. The Constitution gave Congress the right to "establish post offices and post roads." So this use of money from the sale of government-owned land was approved.

Then, in 1806, Congress passed another bill, authorizing the use of federal money to build the National Road. This road would not be in only one state but would cross state lines. And federal money was to be used for a project that seemed to benefit one section of the country more than other sections. There were some statesmen who thought the government had no right to use its money in this way, but others interpreted the act as being in accordance with the Constitution.

This view was generally held by Congress until 1822, when President James Monroe vetoed a bill requesting funds to maintain the National Road. The President did not think Congress had the right to use federal money for this purpose.

At the time of President Monroe's veto, railroads were already being thought about by a few imaginative men. Just three years later, experiments were being carried out with steam locomotives on tracks.

All these events were important in determining whether the federal government should own the railroads. If President Monroe had not vetoed that bill, the government would have embarked on the business of road building and maintenance. And since the railroad was at first generally considered simply another type of road, similar to a turnpike or a post road, the logical result would have been for the government to build and own railroads, particularly those that crossed state lines.

Many railroad enthusiasts advocated this. John Stevens was so convinced that only federal ownership was right that he said, "I shall give no encouragement to private speculations." However, the federal government did not accept this role. Some state governments — notably Pennsylvania — assumed ownership of the lines within their borders. But this was soon given over to private companies. While in most countries the railroads have been entirely the property of the government, in the United States private industry and money built and owned the railroads that helped build the country.

With the question of ownership settled, the next problem was money. Even a very small line cost a large amount. No single individual could bear the heavy burden of such a project. The only alternative was to form a company, plan the railroad, and then get a charter from the state. This charter was necessary before any work could be done. The company could then issue stock to raise the needed money.

To issue stock, a company decides how much its property and rights are worth. Then it sells stock certificates, or shares, to this amount. The certificate owners become partners in the business. If it is honest and prosperous, they share in the profits. If the officials are dishonest or the business a failure, the investors lose their money. In the early days of railroad building, most losses were due to honest failures. As an example, John Charles Frémont, who was a great pathfinder and explorer, was no railroad genius. Once the richest man in California, he died in poverty. He had lost his own fortune and the money of many friends in impossible schemes for building a railroad across the country. Later, dishonest manipulations were to rob many people of their investments while building up the private fortunes of a few.

When the railroads reached the frontier and faced the long stretches of land yet ahead, it became evident that private money could not possibly build the lines needed to serve this vast area. And yet railroads would have to be constructed if the nation were to benefit from the rich territory. It became evident that the government must help in some way.

Since it did not want to own and run the railroads, there were two ways the government might help. It could lend money — as it did in some cases. Or it could do what it did in Ohio — give some of the public lands to be sold to furnish money for the construction of the railway. This method was preferred.

On September 20, 1850, President Millard Fillmore signed the first federal land-grant act. By this act the Illinois Central Railroad was granted a right-of-way and some 2,500,000 acres of public land. This was the first of a series of such land grants, which were to total, in all, more than 131,000,000 acres. Public land, at that time, was selling at $1.25 an acre, with few buyers. The government immediately raised its price to $2.50 an acre for land along the right-of-way where the grant lands lay. The railroads could sell their property at whatever price they could get.

These land grants to the railroads have caused a great deal of discussion and propaganda. Without doubt, they — or some other help — were needed if railroads were to be constructed across the West. Also, they proved to be a good investment for the government, which benefited from having its Western lands settled. And railroads given such grants carried government people and freight at reduced rates. This alone saved the government more than a billion dollars during the next hundred years. The last land grant was made in 1871.

But in spite of the need for them, land grants gave rise to a special kind of cheating. Companies would be formed to lay a railroad in a certain locality. They would get free land and begin to sell it to settlers. These were often foreigners who had no idea of what they were buying, save for the propaganda sent out by the company. Sometimes this land was worthless, impossible for homes. Or the rails would never be laid. So much skulduggery went on that the public grew suspicious of all railroad schemes. But the problem of money for building the long lines West had been partially solved.

One of the problems that had been met in various ways by the different railroad companies was this: How far apart should the rails be? No one knew, so each company solved the problem in its own way.

There were several guideposts. In England, rails were laid 4 feet 8½ inches apart. The English thought they had good reasons for this. All their roads were built to accommodate wagons with wheels set that far apart. Why? Because when they began to build wagons, they already had roads with ruts of that width. These ruts had been made by the chariots of the Romans, who had conquered England in A.D. 43 and occupied it for 300 years. During that time their chariots had left an indelible mark on the roads.

The first locomotives used in America were brought from England. Their wheels fitted rails laid to the 4-foot 8½-inch gauge. So some railroads began laying their rails at that measure.

The builders of the Erie Railroad were thinking big. They laid their tracks 6 feet apart. They thought that this would better accommodate the heavy locomotives they planned to use. In some of the New England valleys, the roadbed was so narrow that rails were placed only 2 or 3 feet apart. Other roads chose 5 feet, or 3½ feet, or any other gauge that suited them. By 1836 thirteen short lines had been built for a total of 162½ miles. Six different gauges had been used.

When Erastus Corning bought the ten lines between Albany and Buffalo to combine them into one system, he found that the variety of gauges was a real nuisance. The same train could not operate straight through until some tracks had been pulled up and others laid down. As railroad companies grew larger, more and more of this sort of thing had to be done.

On July 4, 1862, President Abraham Lincoln signed a bill providing for the construction of a transcontinental railroad. Two companies were named to do the work — the Central Pacific of California was to build eastward; the Union Pacific of Omaha was to lay rails westward. The President was authorized to designate the gauge, for, of course, all rails must be laid to the same width if transcontinental trains were to operate over them.

President Lincoln wanted a 5-foot gauge, but after debate the 4-foot 8½-inch width was decided upon. Following this example, other companies began to adopt that gauge, and in twenty-five years it became the standard gauge for American tracks.

No law governed the matter, and other widths were, and still are, in use on some railroads.

Not only the gauge but the rails themselves had to be considered. A few early railroads in Massachusetts used stone rails and stone crossties, but most of the early lines used wooden rails topped by a flat iron bar about half an inch thick. Such rails had many disadvantages: They wore out quickly and were easily warped or broken, sending the train off the track. One of the worst features was the way the iron bar might come loose and spring back to penetrate the flimsy wooden floor of a car. Sometimes a passenger was caught and impaled on this deadly shaft; always the train was jerked to a stop. Such a sudden stop caused other dangers: Lamps and stoves might be overturned and a fire started. This sort of accident was not uncommon on the short railroads of the East.

Now, with longer runs over isolated lands, wooden rails could no longer be used. And they did not have to be, for by this time iron rails were being manufactured in America. These iron rails had been designed as early as 1830 by Robert L. Stevens, son of the famous John Stevens. Stevens had been sent to England to purchase a locomotive. He had a good deal of time on shipboard to indulge his hobby of whittling. One day his knife shaped a rail which he regarded with satisfaction. He knew that it would be far better than the old wooden rails topped by iron. For though the model was of wood, his whole rail would be made of iron.

The T rail, as it came to be known, was 3½ inches high. The top, or head, flared out from the shaft to a width of 2⅛ inches. The base, 3½ inches wide, could be spiked to the roadbed. Each rail, as Stevens designed it, was 16 feet long, with a fishtail for joining it to the next. It had been the practice to lay the wooden rails on square granite blocks which formed the roadbed. Hewing out the granite blocks was usually the work of convicts. It was a hard, slow, back-breaking job. When Stevens started laying his iron rails on this stone, he found he could proceed faster than the convicts could furnish the blocks. Impatient with the delay, he ordered the workmen to cut logs and square off the rounded sides. This was much faster than shaping granite blocks. Stevens laid these logs crosswise of the roadbed, which was covered with a layer of crushed rock. Then he spiked his rail directly to these ties. They were the first wooden railroad ties in the world.

The inventor was not at all sure that this track would work when an engine with a train of cars was run over it. He didn't know quite what might happen, so he chose to make the trial run himself and was delighted to find that the new type of road was better than the old. It had some give to it that made it more comfortable than the hard stone blocks.

Iron foundries had at first claimed that such a rail could not be manufactured, but Stevens insisted that they try, and finally, under his direction, they produced what he wanted. The rails had to be made in England until 1844. Then American foundries began turning out the now widely used T rail. By 1865 Bessemer steel rails were being produced at the North Chicago Rolling Mills. A larger, heavier modification of the original T rail is standard all over the world today.

The first American railroad signal was a simple affair. A large colored ball was attached to the crossbar of a high pole. This ball could be raised or lowered by hand. The stationmaster had the job of raising the ball high if the track ahead was clear and lowering it if the oncoming train had to stop. This signal was installed on the line of the Delaware Railroad. It gave rise to the term "highball" for a type of signal and to "highballing" for speeding ahead. In time, automatic semaphores replaced this primitive signal device.

On May 24, 1844, Samuel F. B. Morse sent the first message over his telegraph line. No sooner was the Erie Railroad in operation than its superintendent, Charles Minot, saw how valuable the new invention could be in signaling the arrival and departure of trains and in communicating with stations and trains along the line. When the excursion train to Dunkirk developed trouble soon after it started out for the celebration of the completion of the road, Minot tried out the new device. He wired ahead to Port Jervis to have another locomotive ready. The Erie rapidly adopted the telegraph for all sorts of communication. Other lines followed. From the first day it was used by a railroad to the present time, this instrument has been a vital factor in the operation of trains.

As both competition and cooperation increased, many adjustments had to be made between the railroad lines. The various haphazard ways of publishing schedules, issuing tickets, and using hand and lantern signals had to be brought into some sort of harmony. Each of these procedures had to be developed from a primitive, make-do method into an efficient system understood by all. Such improvement was necessary if the railroads were to do their part in building the nation.

And do their part they would, in spite of difficulties, problems, and opposition. There was still much opposition to be ignored or overcome.

Posters like this tried to frighten people into boycotting the "monster" railroad. *Pennsylvania Railroad*

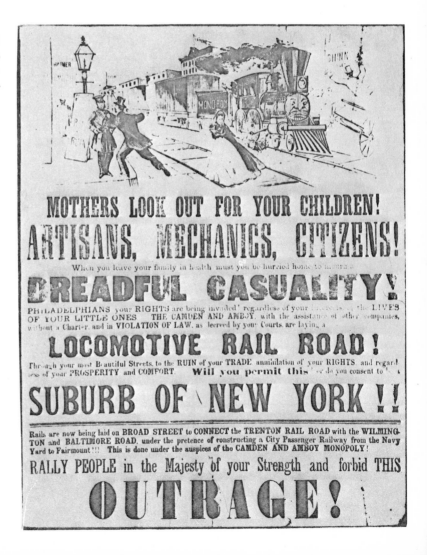

The stagecoach companies that had challenged the Tom Thumb had never given up. Such companies had thousands of dollars invested in animals and equipment. The June Bug line was sending Concord coaches filled with passengers and Conestoga wagons filled with freight over the National Road long before a railroad was in operation. The owners could not see all their money go. Drivers and wagoners could not imagine what they could do when their jobs were no longer needed. They put their fears into song:

> Come, come all you wagoners,
>   Come out, man by man,
> Who's opposed to the rail road
>   Or any such a plan.
>
> I once made my living
>   By driving a team;
> But goods are now hauled
>   On the rail road by steam.
>
> May the devil get the fellow
>   That invented the plan.
> 'Twill ruin all us wagoners
>   And every honest man!

The canalboat owners complained:

> The rail road's a curse on this country, I vow.
> It will ruin us all, and I'm here to say how.
> It's stolen our freight; even taken our horn,
> And given us canawlers good reason to mourn.

The increasing popularity of the trains made travel on Sunday necessary, and this brought complaints from ministers and churches. The railroad companies took this type of complaint very seriously and tried various ways of softening the disapproval. In the 1850's Vermont passed a law requiring the captain to read the Scriptures to the passengers on Sundays. A fancy wrought-iron shelf was put up in each car to hold the special train Bible. It was not uncommon for passengers to hold regular religious services in the cars as they sped along on the Sabbath.

But nothing could stop the progress of the rails across the country.

6

RAILS TO THE MISSISSIPPI

By 1850 much of the experimental work of the railroads had been done. Locomotives, freight and passenger cars, tracks, and road-beds had reached the stage from which the lines could look with confidence toward the West, which at that time meant the land between Buffalo and the Mississippi River. During the next ten years some 20,000 miles of track were laid, and freight and passenger rates decreased. So much mail was carried that postage dropped from ten cents to three cents for letters carried long distances. The entire country was benefiting from the railroads.

Chicago and the Mississippi River beyond it had become the goal of Eastern businessmen with money. Chicago was already recognized as the best junction for rails from north, south, east, and west. Its fortunate location would make it the greatest railroad city in the nation.

All the north-central portion of the country east of the Mississippi was sparsely settled. True, there were cities dotting the land. The Conestogas and Concord stages had already penetrated this rich region. But there were not nearly enough people. Only the faster, more convenient railroads could carry the needed settlers into this wide strip of fertile land. The railroad owners knew this. They knew that both the nation and the railroads would benefit from the development of this area. They began to lay rails westward.

An earlier chapter described how the Pennsylvania Railroad set out for Pittsburgh and the business of shipping the products of the booming steel city. Now the owners looked farther West. They leased a line that ran from Pittsburgh to Chicago, so they had a continuous road from Philadelphia to the "Junction City."

Not to be outdone by its rival, the Baltimore and Ohio helped finance the building of a railroad from its terminal at Wheeling westward and northward to Chicago.

St. Louis had had a railroad since 1852, but the locomotive had been shipped by boat up the Mississippi. The westward-looking Baltimore and Ohio, seeing that other lines were competing for the Northern trade, began to make connections with lines to St. Louis, with an eye to the growing Southwest.

So far the Mississippi had not been bridged. This feat was not to be accomplished by the great Eastern lines but was to be the result of the building of two small railroads in the North.

In 1847 Rock Island, Illinois, was a little village on the eastern bank of the Mississippi. John Deere had just brought to it his plow factory from Grand Detour, and the town was looking forward to rapid industrial growth. But to achieve this, a railroad would be needed. So the Rock Island and La Salle Railroad was incorporated.

Across from Rock Island was another small, ambitious town, Davenport, Iowa. There were close ties between the two settlements.

The Iowa town had been named for Colonel George Davenport of Rock Island. In a tiff over the actions of his neighbors, the colonel had left his home and with a Canadian Indian companion had crossed the river and laid out his own village. The people of Davenport were as interested in the Rock Island and La Salle Railroad as were their friends in Illinois. The road was surveyed, but little else was done during the next four years.

By 1851, however, Eastern railroad builders were eyeing the Mississippi region. An interested group revived the original line, renamed it the Chicago and Rock Island, and sent out John B. Jervis to be president of the line. Jervis, as has been related in a previous chapter, had brought the Stourbridge Lion to America from England in 1829. He had been engaged in railroading ever since. The construction of the line began at Chicago and proceeded westward toward Rock Island.

One of the first interesting anecdotes connected with the line occurred on October 10, 1852, when 40 miles of rails had been laid to Joliet, Illinois. The locomotive Rocket had just arrived from New Jersey. It was placed in front of six bright new yellow passenger cars filled with enthusiastic rooters. It made the trip to Joliet in two hours. But alas! No turntable had been provided at Joliet. The train could not turn around, so it had to back the entire 40 miles of the return to Chicago.

Meanwhile, the people of Davenport had decided that they must have a railroad if their neighbors across the river had one. They chartered the Mississippi and Missouri Railroad. It was the custom to choose two geographical names, usually the intended terminals of the line, and to link them in the name of the new company. Since this line originated in a Mississippi River town, the first part of the name was logical. The second part may have been wishful thinking. Anyway, construction began toward the river.

The idea of linking the two cities — Rock Island and Davenport — by a bridge had been simmering for some time. Now with the two railroads approaching the river, such a bridge became still more desirable. So when the Illinois tracks reached Rock Island, work began on the bridge.

Across the river, the Mississippi and Missouri was heading south and east toward the busy steamboat landing and lumber town of Muscatine. But Iowa City was the capital of the state, and it thought it should not be denied the benefits of a railroad. Officials of the city offered the railroad owners $50,000 if they would build their line to the capital. There was one condition: A train must enter the city by midnight of December 31, 1855.

The race began, for the railroad needed that $50,000. But work as hard as they could, it looked as if the prize would be lost. An Iowa winter set in, ground was frozen, and blizzards swept howling across the bleak land. The last few days were a frenzied nightmare, but the thirty-first came, and the city had not been reached. All day long the men worked, and at five in the afternoon the rails were still 1,000 feet from the city.

The thermometer dropped to zero and below. As night fell, bonfires were built to provide light and warmth for the workers. The city officials and businessmen came out. Wrapped in mufflers and overcoats, they pitched in. Ties were laid, rails were spiked down, and each sledge stroke was echoed by a cheer from the watching crowd. And at 11:30 p.m. — just a half hour before the deadline — the rails reached the city limits.

The locomotive was waiting just behind the workmen. The

73

engineer and fireman, who had been laying rails with the others, ran back and leaped to their places. The engineer opened the throttle; the fireman piled wood on the blaze. Nothing happened. The engine was frozen to the tracks. There was no time to waste. Chains were brought and hooked to the front of the balky locomotive. Some stout fellows took iron bars and pried at the wheels; others surrounded the engine and pushed with all their might. And so the reluctant "train" was pulled and pushed and dragged across the line that marked the city's boundary just as the bells rang out the old year and rang in the new. Iowa City had its railroad; the company had won its $50,000.

Meanwhile, the first Mississippi River bridge was being constructed. The cornerstone had been laid in September, 1854. The work was completed on April 21, 1856. The next day the locomotive Fort Des Moines puffed its way over the bridge — the first Iron Horse to cross the Mississippi under its own power.

For some years Iowa City was the end of the line westward. Thousands were brought this far by railroad, to continue their journey by wagon or on foot. Here, in 1856, 1,300 Mormon converts from Europe camped while they built their wooden-wheeled pushcarts for the 1,000-mile trip farther on to Utah. As they plodded along, they must have thought with longing of the railroad behind them. But they sang:

> For some must push and some must pull
> As we go marching up the hill;
> So merrily on our way we go
> Until we reach the Valley-o!

All the railroad lines pushing toward the Mississippi carried settlers to build up the interior regions of the country. But one line set an example that many others followed in the years to come. This line was the Illinois Central, the first with a definite campaign to encourage settlers to ride its cars to new homes.

When Congress granted this company its 2,500,000 acres of land in Illinois, it was to enable the railroad to raise money by selling the land to settlers. In this way both the railroad and the country would benefit. At this time the United States did not have immigration quotas. People were needed to fill up and develop the land, and they had to be found outside this country and encouraged to come here.

The Illinois Central was to do just that. It was to run from the Wisconsin border down through the central part of the state to Cairo at the southern tip near the Missouri border, at the confluence of the Wabash and the Mississippi. This was sparsely settled country, but rich farmland. It would be attractive to settlers, once the road was in operation.

There were difficulties, however. There was, as yet, no rail connection with the East, and all supplies such as materials, food, and even labor had to be brought in over the complicated system of rails and canals and rivers. And labor was scarce. All over the country railroads were being built, and the demand for railroad laborers was far greater than the supply.

Advertisements were placed in the newspapers of the leading Eastern cities, posters were pasted on walls and in horsecars, and agents set up headquarters to help men make their way to Illinois. Wages of $1.25 a day and constant work were offered. Married men were encouraged to take their families and plan to settle there, where workers were needed, the atmosphere was uncontaminated by city crowds, and living was cheap. The campaign was successful; the main line was finished by September 21, 1856.

WANTED!
3,000 LABORERS

On the 12th Division of the

ILLINOIS CENTRAL RAILROAD

Wages, $1.25 per Day.

Fare, from New-York, only - - $4 75

By Railroad and Steamboat, to the work in the
State of Illinois.

Constant employment for two years or more given. Good board can be obtained at two dollars per week.

This is a rare chance for persons to go West, being sure of permanent employment in a healthy climate, where land can be bought cheap, and for fertility is not surpassed in any part of the Union.

Men with families preferred.

For further information in regard to it. call at the Central Railroad Office,

173 BROADWAY,
CORNER OF COURTLANDT ST.

NEW-YORK.

R. B. MASON, Chief Engineer.

H. PHELPS, AGENT,

JULY, 1853.

The building of the Illinois Central railroad required recruiting manpower from throughout the United States and from many European countries. Reproduced here is an 1853 advertisement calling for 3,000 laborers. During the construction period (1851–56) the Illinois Central brought 100,000 people to Illinois to work on the railroad and to settle the lands along the line. *Illinois Central Railroad*

An Illinois Central Railroad land office at the turn of the century. This office sold land in the railroad's territory in the Yazoo Valley for $8 an acre. Buyers were given six years to pay for the land. *Illinois Central System*

dred thousand of these posters were mailed to people, especially farmers, in the East and South. They were nailed up in post offices, Atlantic steamship terminals, and wherever Du Puy thought they would catch the eye of a prospective buyer.

The posters were supplemented by advertisements in leading newspapers and by announcements in the pamphlets published for the guidance of immigrants. Every possible success story was funneled to Eastern papers to lure those who put little trust in advertise-

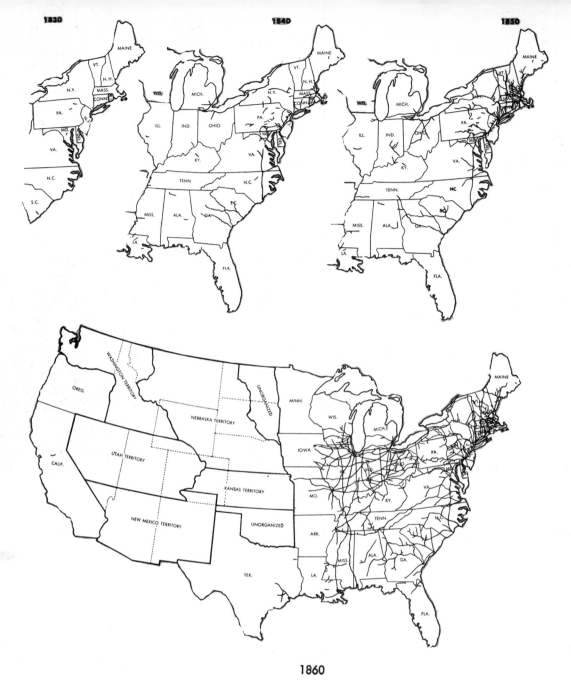

1860

This series of maps shows the growth of American railroads from 1830 to 1880. During the first ten years, completed lines increased from 23 to 2,808 miles. During the next ten years 6,200 more miles were laid. From 1850 to 1860 much of the settled

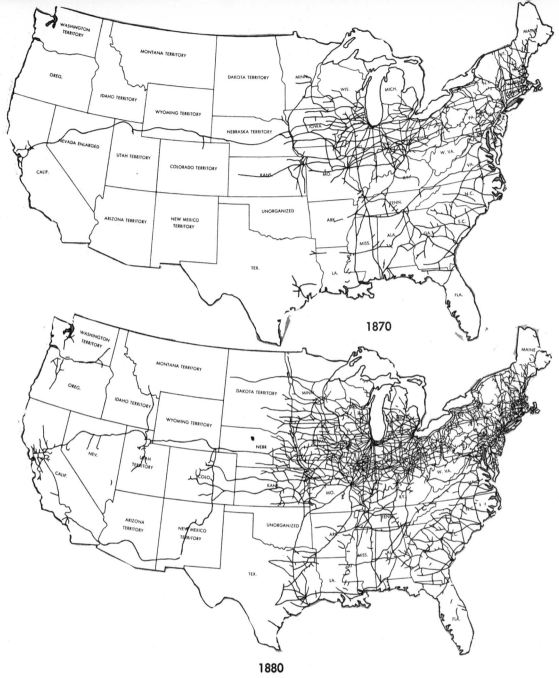

1870

1880

part of the country saw railroad development as 30,626 miles of track were opened to travel. In 1870 there were 52,922 miles, and in 1880 the mileage had reached 93,267 miles, with two lines reaching the Pacific Coast. *Association of American Railroads*

ments. Du Puy's imagination did not stop here. He prepared and distributed thousands of pamphlets illustrated with woodcuts showing happy settlers and filled with glowing accounts of the country.

All this had its effect. New England farmers, weary of fighting the rocky soil, began to come in such numbers that those who stayed behind were alarmed. Prices of farmland in those states began to drop, and counterpropaganda campaigns were begun. But the New Englanders came on, establishing many towns to which they gave their distinctive Yankee flavor. Other groups came from the South, from New York, and Pennsylvania.

But not enough Americans came to settle all those millions of acres. An office was opened in New York City with runners to wait at the docks and talk immigrants into going on to Illinois. The company offered a low fare of only $4.75 from New York to Chicago, and the runners impressed on the newcomers the advantages of proceeding immediately to the wonderful region.

It was not easy to convince the newcomers. Europeans had been warned that they might be met by crooks and all their possessions taken from them. This had been done for years, and disclosure of the evil practice had been used by several European countries as a threat to keep their people from running off to the Promised Land. The runners for the Illinois Central were not crooks, but they had to overcome the suspicion of the immigrants. Men of good, but not flashy, appearance were employed for the delicate job. Some could speak German or one of the Scandinavian languages. The Scandinavians were especially wary, for many of their countrymen had been fleeced upon arrival by the scoundrels that infested the docks.

The Illinois Central managers saw that many Swedes were going to Minnesota and Wisconsin, so they sent Oscar Malmborg to

Sweden to urge discontented farmers to come to Illinois. Many Germans, too, were settling in Wisconsin, so the Illinois Central sent Francis Hoffman to Germany to deflect the tide down to Illinois. He was so persuasive that in two years some 2,000 Germans came to settle on the company's lands.

The railroad sold most of the land it wished to get rid of. Countless new settlements were established, and the state, which had been almost bankrupt in 1851, was prospering in 1861.

Other railroads in the state had seen what the Illinois Central was doing and had inaugurated active campaigns for settlers for the land they had to sell. And not only to Illinois but to the whole interior — the West of that time — railroad propaganda was bringing immigrants to build the country.

It was not all sweetness and light. Many roughnecks and loafers rode the trains into the frontier lands. Many were lazy and shiftless; many were evil. Bands of outlaws formed to rob the people, to strip the forests of timber, and to steal from the newly established factories and mills. But most of the immigrants were sturdy farmers from the East and from Europe — people who had found life too difficult in their old homes or who had been crowded out by grasping landowners. They came seeking a bit of land they could call their own — a home. And they were willing to work for it. These people would be the backbone of the strip of states along the eastern shore of the Mississippi River — the first states actually built by the railroads.

7

RAILROADS HELP SAVE THE UNION

When newly elected President Abraham Lincoln left his home in Springfield, Illinois, for his inauguration in Washington, D.C., he spoke to the crowd of well-wishers bidding him good-bye. To do so, he stood on the rear platform of the railroad car that was to carry him on the first leg of his journey. In doing this, Lincoln started a custom that has survived for 100 years — the politicians' practice of addressing crowds from rear platforms of railroad cars.

This was on February 11, 1861. Nearly 28 years earlier, Andrew Jackson had been the first President of the United States to ride on a train. President Jackson's trip had been the 13 miles from Baltimore to Ellicott's Mills, over the Baltimore and Ohio line. President-elect Lincoln would journey some 700 miles, over several different lines. During those few intervening years the railroads had become a vital part of American life. During the next 5 years they would help preserve the Union.

Even during the next few days they did their part in saving Lincoln's life. He had been informed by the detective Allan Pinkerton that a plot was afoot to assassinate him in Baltimore. Because of this warning, Lincoln kept his journey as secret as possible. A special train raced across Pennsylvania at night, with Lincoln in a darkened car. When the train had to stop for water, his companions could escape to get a bite of supper, but the great man had to be content with the meager roll and tea they brought back to him.

The train reached the Baltimore station of the Philadelphia, Wilmington and Baltimore line. Then the sleeping car carrying Lincoln was drawn by horses through the dark streets to the depot of the Washington line. There the special party had to wait two hours, because the Washington train was late. Lincoln, sitting in the darkened car, could hear rowdies at the station singing Rebel songs, unaware that the man who was to hold the Union together was sitting nearby. Finally, the Washington train arrived, Lincoln was secretly put aboard, and the rest of the journey was made in safety.

News pictures and cartoons of this "cops and robbers" trip depicted it in various ways. But in all the illustrations the train played a conspicuous part.

On April 14, only a few weeks after Lincoln's inauguration, the Confederate flag was hoisted over Fort Sumter, South Carolina. A heavy bombardment had forced the federal troops to withdraw. The Civil War had begun. On April 15, President Lincoln declared a state of war and called for troops to defend the Union. On the same day he took over certain railroads to make sure that troops and supplies could be moved as needed. Massachusetts, far to the north, was the first state to answer this call. Just four days later, the Massachusetts Sixth Regiment, carried by train to Baltimore, was attacked by a mob in the streets of that city.

At noon on April 25 the plaintive wail of a locomotive whistle announced the arrival in Washington of the train bringing the New York Seventh Regiment. They had come under difficulties. Angry mobs had tried to prevent their arrival by tearing up the tracks and burning the bridges along the line. But the Union troops had relaid and rebuilt them and had come on.

Thus, within ten days, the role of the railroads had been set: They would move troops and supplies; and they would be torn up in the attempt to destroy their usefulness. Both sides were to use the railroads — the first time railroads ever played an important part in warfare. But the South was at a disadvantage: It had fewer miles of tracks than the North; between lines there were gaps, such as the 40 miles between Danville, Virginia, and Greensboro, North Carolina. This was on an important route for the Confederate Army. Jefferson Davis, president of the Confederacy, saw how valuable it would be to have this gap bridged by rails, and as early as November of the first year of the war, he urged that this be done. It was not accomplished until May, 1864. Moreover, the South did not have the materials or the factories to produce rails and engines to replace those destroyed by Union troops.

The federal government, on the other hand, could command thousands of miles of track. Steel mills in Pittsburgh and Chicago were busy rolling rails and manufacturing locomotives. The Baltimore and Ohio, with its connecting lines to St. Louis, tied this city to the North. This shattered the South's hopes of getting supplies from the West over the Mississippi Railroad. This demonstrates how important the railroads were in the conflict and how much they did to preserve the Union. Individual events were to emphasize this importance.

One of the earliest effective blows was struck by the Confederate the train and watch their chance to steal the locomotive and run it up to the North.

It was a daring scheme, but if it proved successful, it would cut an important line of communication between the two Southern cities. The Union men, dressed as civilians, boarded the train at Atlanta, and away it went. At the little town of Big Shanty the train stopped to take on water. This gave the crew a chance to get some breakfast. They left the cars and went into a small, trackside restaurant, fol-

This is the historic locomotive The General, object of the famous Andrews' Raid. It is pictured with wood in the tender, since that was the original fuel it burned. It was later converted to coal and then to diesel oil. *Louisville and Nashville Railroad*

lowed by most of the passengers. This was what Andrews' men were counting on. They speedily uncoupled the locomotive and the three front boxcars, mounted the cab, and set the General speeding northward.

Inside the restaurant, conductor W. A. Fuller and engineer Jeff Cain looked out the window to see their locomotive disappearing. Immediately they understood what had happened. They dashed outside and started running up the track after their engine. For two miles they loped along the track, but it seemed a hopeless race. They were losing ground — and breath. Then they came upon a track crew with a handcar. As the raiders had passed this crew they had taken away their tools and cut the telegraph wire so no message could be sent ahead to stop them. Fuller and Cain took the handcar and set out again. They were pumping the handcar for all they were worth, soaked by rain and perspiration, but desperately hurrying along, when they came to a rail loosened by the raiders. Before the two men could stop the handcar, it had been sent hurtling off the track. It took almost superhuman effort to get the car back on the rails beyond the broken section.

When they came to Etowah station, they found an old yard engine, the Yonah, standing on a sidetrack. They got this onto the main line, picked up a crew of Confederate soldiers, and started off again, determined to recover the stolen locomotive.

Ahead of the pursuers, the raiders had come upon a train blocking their way. It was waiting for another train to pass. Andrews boldly stepped down from the cab and ordered the crew of the obstructing train to clear the tracks. The men were suspicious, but Andrews showed such authority that they obeyed, though it took them an hour. That hour cost the raiders most of their lead in the desperate race. Fuller, in the little old Yonah, was catching up. Aware that this must be so, Andrews stopped to take up another section of track and cut the telegraph wires again.

Fuller had almost caught up with the raiders when the broken track stopped him again. He abandoned the Yonah and took after the General on foot. Then he had a bit of luck. He met a southbound freight train, drawn by the plucky little Texas. There was no way to turn this train around to head north after the General, so Fuller put the engine in reverse and set out, flying backward up the track after the escaping General. Andrews uncoupled two of the boxcars so he could go faster, and he left them on the track to delay the Texas. Fuller's crew pushed these boxcars aside and went on with the chase. The little freight engine was making good time and soon came in sight of its quarry. Andrews set fire to his last boxcar and left it on a bridge. But the sturdy little Texas just pushed the burning car off the track and sped on.

The Confederate engine was gaining on the raiders when Andrews ran out of fuel. He could go no farther. So he ordered his men to put the General in reverse so it would run backward down the track and smack into its pursuer. Then each man was to jump and run.

The chase was over. It had been dramatic and exciting while it lasted, and though the Union raiders did not succeed in stealing the Confederate train and in interrupting Confederate communications, the daring and ingenuity of both groups captured the interest of the country. The two famous locomotives have been preserved for history lovers to admire. The General is on view in the Union Station at Chattanooga; the Texas stands in Grant Park in Atlanta.

Less spectacular but more successful was the raid on the Memphis and Charleston Railroad at Huntsville, Alabama. The Union forces captured the yards, shops, and trains of this line, cutting off a vital supply line of the Confederacy.

In the spring of 1862 the Confederate forces were put under the command of General Robert E. Lee. A West Point graduate and a wise and skillful soldier, General Lee at once began to make good use of what railroads the South could command. At this time the federal armies began their campaign against Richmond, Virginia, the new Confederate capital. Both armies used every car they could get hold of to move troops, supplies, and equipment to this vital area. Stonewall Jackson's entire army was transported by rail from the Shenandoah Valley to Richmond.

The Northern forces were working out some strange and ingenious ways to make their trains more powerful as military weapons. Guns were mounted on specially built cars with a protection in front

This mortar was mounted on a flatcar. It was used by federal artillery forces at the siege of Petersburg. It fired a 200-pound shell. *Association of American Railroads*

This specially built car carried a heavy mortar from which shells weighing 200 pounds bombarded Southern strongholds. This was the first use of railroad tracks for the movement of such heavy war weapons. *Library of Congress*

to shelter the soldiers as they moved to advance positions. Other cars carried mortars weighing as much as 17,000 pounds and firing 200 rounds of shells. Such heavy equipment could scarcely have been moved without rails and steam engines. Some cars were covered with metal armor to protect them from the guns of the enemy.

And hospital trains — the first in the world — were being designed and built. At first the sick and wounded were just piled into boxcars to be taken to the hospitals set up behind the lines or in a nearby city. Before very long, specially designed and equipped cars

An artist's sketch shows how the wounded were loaded onto flatcars to be transported from the battlefield to a hospital. Later specially equipped cars were used for this purpose. *Library of Congress*

were used. These had rows of bunks suspended by heavy elastic bands. These cars advanced to the very front of battle and evacuated the wounded men quickly and efficiently. Not as quickly and efficiently as today's helicopters, of course. But 100 years ago this service seemed to be a miracle of progress.

By 1864 much of the railroad systems of the South was either destroyed or in the hands of Northern troops. With shops and stations, tracks and trains gone, the Confederacy was helpless to withstand the battering of the Union armies. For by this time the U.S. Military Railway Service was so well organized that it was supporting every move of the North's forces. Even when Confederate soldiers destroyed rails or bridges, McCallum's men rebuilt them so fast that it was discouraging to the South. When the Southern forces were unable to stop General Sherman in his campaign against Atlanta, a Confederate soldier grumbled, "Oh, what's the use? Don't you know

94

that Sherman carries along a duplicate tunnel?" It seemed as if, when an installation was destroyed, the general just pulled another out of his pocket and set it in place. For four months Sherman's 100,000 men and 35,000 horses and mules were furnished food, ammunition, and supplies over 473 miles of single-track railroad from Louisville to Atlanta.

The railroads had one more sad duty to perform in relation to this period of the country's history. After President Lincoln was assassinated, in April, 1865, his body was returned to Springfield, Illinois, on a special funeral train. As it crossed the country from Washington, thousands of mourners stood along the tracks or waited in railroad stations to show their respect to the dead leader. The poet, Walt Whitman, described this mournful journey:

> Over the breast of the spring, the land and cities,
> Amid lanes and through old woods, where lately the violets
>   peeped from the ground, spotting the gray debris, . . .
>
>   .   .   .   .   .
>
> Passing the apple tree blows of white and pink in the
>   orchards,
> Carrying a corpse to where it shall rest in the grave,
> Night and day journeys a coffin.

The railroads had done much toward building the country during their short existence of fewer than forty years. Now they had proved that they could help preserve that country as one unified nation.

8

FROM SEA TO SHINING SEA

Now that the question of the Union had been settled, the railroads could get back to the business of building up the country. One of the first things to be done was the laying of tracks into the far West. There had to be a system of continuous rails so that trains could run from the Atlantic to the Pacific.

This was no new idea. Long before there were any steam locomotives puffing across New York or Pennsylvania, long before men had learned how to cross the Alleghenies, people were dreaming of conquering not only the 2,000-feet-high Eastern mountains, but the far more formidable Rockies and Sierra Nevada.

As early as February 6, 1832, an article in a Michigan newspaper suggested that a steam railroad be built from New York City to the Oregon coast. The article was unsigned, perhaps because the author feared he would be considered crazy to suggest such a thing.

In 1835 the Reverend Samuel Parker went to the Oregon country as a missionary to the Indians. He made his way over the Rocky Mountains by means of South Pass, in what is now south-central Wyoming. This easy route had been discovered some ten years earlier by two famous mountain men, Jedediah Smith and Tom Fitzpatrick. When the Reverend Parker wrote about his own journey West, he declared that South Pass offered no real obstacle to the building of a steam railway.

Such accounts and predictions fired the imaginations of several enterprising Easterners. One of these was the explorer John Charles Frémont. He was so sure that trains could get over the Rockies, even in midwinter, that he set out in the fall of 1848 to prove his point. He did not favor the northern route over the South Pass but chose to explore the possibilities of a road over the mountains in what is now southern Colorado. It was a disastrous expedition that cost the dreamer the lives of eleven of his party and more than $10,000 worth of equipment. These were among the first deaths to be charged to the building of a transcontinental railroad.

In spite of the tragic outcome of this venture, Frémont could not give up his idea. Then, in 1853, the government ordered five different surveys to be made to determine the best route over the mountains. Each survey was to be along a different parallel of latitude. By this time the government was so interested in the project that it was willing to spend money on it. Jefferson Davis, the Secretary of War, favored the most southerly route. This would have had to cross the deserts of Texas, New Mexico, and Arizona to end somewhere near, or at, San Diego, California. Mr. Davis had few supporters of his plan. Frémont was still strong for his own favored route. He had taken an enormous fortune from his gold mines in California, and he poured much of this into promoting a railroad through southern Colorado. As a result, he lost not only his own fortune but the investments made by those who trusted his judgment. And there were many who eagerly promoted the idea of a railroad over the South Pass.

Congress was in favor of a railroad to the Pacific, but it could not agree on where the road should be. The South was sure that the North would get the route and that the Southern states would not benefit from it. The North, even then, was far more thickly populated than the South. One Southern Senator grumbled that a north-routed railroad would pour "all its vast travel and freight into the northern states and cities." He felt that this question, rather than slavery, was vital enough to justify the Southern states in seceding from the Union and building their own Confederacy.

The question was bitterly debated until on July 4, 1862, President Lincoln signed the Pacific Railroad Act, which provided for the construction of a railroad from the Mississippi to the Pacific. Two companies were named to do the work: the Union Pacific and the Central Pacific. These two companies were created by Congress for this particular purpose. Federal money and resources would be lent to help them do the job. The Union Pacific was to build westward from a point on the northern edge of the Platte River Valley in the Territory of Nebraska — near where Kearney, Nebraska, now stands — to the western boundary of the Territory of Nevada. The Central Pacific was to build eastward from the West Coast to where it would meet the Union Pacific.

Of all the events in the exciting story of the American railroads, this has been most often told. The driving of the golden spike at Promontory, Utah, on May 10, 1869, must, of course, be included in any account of American railroads. It has inspired many books, songs, anecdotes, and biographies. And tragedies, scandals, and disasters. For it was the great epic of railroad building — the dream of the

98

National Road spelled out in shining rails and puffing steam locomotives, in new cities and industries, in marvels of engineering skill and the dogged determination of laborers.

The Central Pacific started work first. On January 8, 1863, Governor Leland Stanford of California stood in a wagon box on a muddy Sacramento street and shoveled dry earth down onto the slime. This was the beginning of the embankment that was to carry the rails out of the state capital. In May, work on the first stretch from Sacramento to Placerville was begun.

A look at a map of the United States shows that the Union Pacific had undertaken to construct well over 1,000 miles of road, while the Central Pacific was committed to fewer than 200 miles, under the first plan. This was altered, so that in the end the Union Pacific laid 1,086 miles of track and the Central Pacific 690 miles. The 400-mile difference was more than made up by the Sierra Nevada which the Western company had to scale.

Most people thought this could not be done. But there was one young railroad engineer who knew it was possible. He was Theodore Judah, called Crazy Judah because of his insistence that it was feasible to build a railroad over the Sierras.

Theodore Judah was born in Connecticut in March, 1826. His life had matched the development of the railroads. When he entered young manhood, he began to study engineering. Before he was twenty, he had surveyed railroad routes in his home state and in Massachusetts. From then on he proved his ability by building several railroads in the East. When Judah was twenty-seven, he was recommended by Horatio Seymour, the governor of New York, as the most competent railroad builder in the East. He was suggested as the very man to build a short railroad in California, from the rich diggings near Folsom to Sacramento.

Judah accepted the job, took his bride to the coast, and within a year had completed the 21-mile road. This was early in 1856. The talk at this time was of a transcontinental railroad, and Judah began his campaign for a route across the Sierras. He went to Washington in 1859 with his plans, but the threat of the coming war between the states was taking the attention of Congress, and the young man's enthusiasm was wasted. It was to be three years before the Pacific Railroad Act was passed.

Judah returned to California and turned from talking of a transcontinental road to advocating a good road to the Comstock in Nevada, where the big silver boom was on. He managed to interest four businessmen in the project. These men, soon to be known as the Big Four, were Collis P. Huntington, and Mark Hopkins, partners in a hardware store; Leland Stanford, a lawyer and grocer; and Charles

This sign at Goldfield, Nevada, gives the tourist some facts about this mining town. It shows that one carload of ore brought down from the Comstock was worth more than half a million dollars.

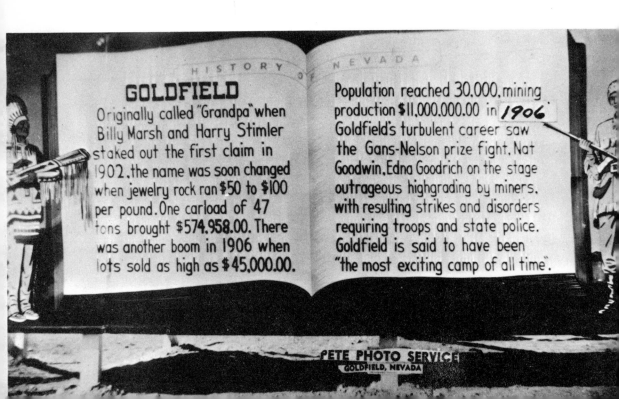

HISTORY OF NEVADA

GOLDFIELD

Originally called "Grandpa" when Billy Marsh and Harry Stimler staked out the first claim in 1902. the name was soon changed when jewelry rock ran $50 to $100 per pound. One carload of 47 tons brought $574,958.00. There was another boom in 1906 when lots sold as high as $45,000.00.

Population reached 30,000, mining production $11,000,000.00 in 1906 Goldfield's turbulent career saw the Gans-Nelson prize fight. Nat Goodwin, Edna Goodrich on the stage outrageous highgrading by miners. with resulting strikes and disorders requiring troops and state police. Goldfield is said to have been "the most exciting camp of all time".

PETE PHOTO SERVICE
GOLDFIELD, NEVADA

Crocker, a dry goods merchant. They put up the money, which, added to what Judah and his friends contributed, gave them enough to start the work.

Judah now realized that he could make a more successful appeal to Congress if he urged a very practical reason for his pet scheme. So in 1861, with the Civil War an actuality, he went back to Washington with the plea that the railroad was needed as a war measure to keep California and Nevada, with their rich gold and silver mines, in the Union. It took him a full year to persuade Congress, but he finally succeeded, obtaining generous land grants and loans of millions of dollars. Now his friends in California no longer called him crazy. Instead, he was hailed as a genius.

Judah was a visionary who wanted to build a railroad, no matter what it might cost in money and effort. The Big Four wanted to make money. The two aims were not the same, and Judah found he could not work with his former associates. They paid him $100,000, and he left California for the East. But he contracted yellow fever at Panama and died a week after reaching New York. Though he was the man responsible for obtaining the commission to build the Western section of the road, the Big Four took over and carried out Judah's plan. They also carried out their own wishes and became very rich. Their names are found in the names of universities, libraries and other institutions, and of streets and buildings throughout California. Judah is commemorated chiefly by an unpretentious monument in Sacramento.

Samuel S. Montague was employed to take Judah's place as chief engineer. He faced a tremendous task. The Sierra Nevada has a core of solid granite. In some places tunnels had to be bored through this rock. The lowest possible pass was at an altitude of 7,000 feet,

This locomotive, the C. P. Huntington, was shipped around the Horn to California, where it was first used in 1864. *Southern Pacific Company*

where the snow lay 50 feet deep in winter. There were sheer precipices to be scaled and deep gorges to be bridged somehow. The road had to be so constructed that the upward grade would be no more than 140 feet to a mile, so locomotives could pull a train of cars over it.

The mountains were the worst problem, but after they were crossed, a dreadful desert lay ahead. Here workmen suffered from the heat and lack of water.

Only 18 miles of track were laid in 1863; only 12 miles the next year. By May, 1865, 56 miles of track had reached the Sierra foothills. Sturdy locomotives were hauling passengers at ten cents per mile, freight at fifteen cents per ton per mile. The completed section had all the business it could handle.

Labor was scarce. The company could not find enough men to keep the rails moving ahead. Finally, it was decided to use some of the Chinese miners who were working over the streambeds abandoned by white gold hunters. When someone asked how the Chinese, weighing around 100 pounds each, could build a railroad over the mountain, he was told, "They built the Great Wall of China, didn't they? That was a tough job, too!"

So the Chinese were hired, and they set to work, an odd-looking crew of railroad stiffs in basket hats and pigtails, blue blouses, and loose pantaloons. By 1866, 6,000 Chinese were swarming up and down the slopes. Thousands had been shipped in from China. They were tireless and fearless as they carved out a road for the tracklayers to follow. At places they were lowered over the cliffs in baskets. There, swinging between blue sky and green abyss, they chiseled out of the granite face a path on which others could stand to hew a ledge wide enough for the rails.

Winter posed other problems such as the 50-foot snowdrifts, the cold and the wind and the sleet. During the summer of 1867 miles of snowsheds were constructed to cover the tracks and the workers. By 1869, trains were running for 40 miles through the long semi-

This sketch shows the Chinese workers watching a Central Pacific train emerge from one snow shed and approach another. *Association of American Railroads*

darkness of the barnlike sheds. Snowplows were developed to whirl the snow from the tracks ahead of workmen and locomotives. The first plows were not very successful against the heavy drifts, but in time an efficient plow was devised and put to work.

On and on, up the western face of the Sierras climbed the narrow pathway. Twenty-eight miles lay ahead to the rich diggings at Dutch Flat, where Theodore Judah had planned to start his road over the mountains. Above this tiny settlement rose the pass over which the tragic Donner-Reed party had made its way in 1846. Here, at Donner Pass, in the winter of 1866, it seemed almost as if they could go no farther. Supplies, which had been brought up by sleds drawn by oxteams, could no longer reach the workmen. Many of the Chinese were freezing and had to be sent down to Sacramento to save their lives. Others dug down under the snowdrifts and eked out a miserable two months, almost starved to death. Work stopped for a while.

When a snowplow was not enough, tracks were cleared by hand. C. William Witbeck

But spring returned, and 15,000 Chinese were brought up to continue the interrupted labor. Most of these new workers had been brought from their homeland to supplement those already here. By summer the rails stretched for 94 miles to come smack against the granite cliffs, where fifteen tunnels must be driven through rock so hard that picks and chisels crumbled against it. Even dynamite, that powerful explosive just discovered by a Swede named Alfred Nobel, was of little use. However, a new, more powerful formula was worked out by a Swedish chemist who called this explosive nitroglycerine.

The stuff was tried and found to be unexpectedly effective. It blasted a crew of Chinese so completely that their bodies were never recovered. After this experience, nitroglycerine was treated with greater respect and caution.

The crews reached the crest and blasted out Summit Tunnel, a quarter of a mile long through the granite core of the mountain. It took a whole year to bore this tunnel — with thousands of Chinese working twelve-hour shifts, day and night, from both ends and in both directions from a shaft sunk straight down to the middle. Four crews, working around the clock, with sweat streaming and muscles straining, could cut through only eight inches a day. This proved to be the most expensive quarter mile in all railroad history.

While all this tremendous labor was going on in the California mountains, the Union Pacific was moving westward from Nebraska. Ground had been broken on December 3, 1863, in the Missouri River bottoms at Omaha, Nebraska. Financial troubles delayed the work, and it was not until July 10, 1865, that the first rail was laid.

General Grenville M. Dodge was chief engineer during most of the construction of this line. While mountains and snows daunted the Central Pacific crews, Indians, grasshoppers, and blizzards plagued the Union Pacific. The Cheyenne and Sioux were not willing to have their lands invaded by the snorting Iron Horse. General Dodge complained that "every mile had to be run within the range of a rifle."

There were other difficulties. The soft cottonwood trees of the region required special treatment to make them suitable for ties. And 6,250,000 ties were needed. Thousands of tons of iron rails and their fittings, the materials and equipment for building bridges, and all the supplies for the laborers had to be brought by wagon and oxteam from the railroad in Iowa or by flatboat up the Missouri River.

Samuel B. Reed, general superintendent and engineer of construction for the Union Pacific Railroad, looks over the grading before the ties are laid for the first transcontinental railroad. *Union Pacific Railroad*

This shows a Union Pacific construction train, with the open truck car carrying rails and the boxcars with equipment. The train crew lined up for this 1868 photograph. *Union Pacific Railroad*

Nevertheless, some 10 miles of track were laid in the first two months after the work got under way. Forty miles were laid during 1865. By the end of 1867 the summit of the Rockies had been reached at Sherman Hill, some 8,247 feet above sea level. The Union Pacific line was more than 500 miles long. In 1868 another 430 miles of track were laid.

The work on the Union Pacific was done chiefly by Irish laborers. As the rails crept West, many Mormons from the settlements in Utah and Wyoming joined the crews to benefit from the wages paid. All began work at daylight, after an early breakfast. Bridge-building gangs went ahead of the track crews. Surveyors and road graders came next, with the tracklayers last. Rails were brought to the end of the line on open truck cars. Teams of five men on each side unloaded the rails. When the foreman shouted, "Down!" a rail was pulled from the truck and lowered to the ties, which were already in place. As the rails hit the ties, a workman measured the gauge; then came the men to pound in the spikes that held the rails firmly in place. About 2 miles of track could be laid in a day on fairly level ground.

The crews traveled alongside the rails in large boxlike cars which served as their homes. These made a sort of moving town which became known as Hell on Wheels because of the disturbances

This photograph of Sherman Station, Wyoming, was taken by the photographer J. W. Jackson in 1870. *Union Pacific Railroad Museum Collection*

it caused. For not only train crews but also saloonkeepers, gamblers, and gunmen followed the tracks. They often became troublesome, as they tried in one way or another to get hold of the wages earned by the laborers. In 1867 General Dodge had to call in the soldiers from nearby Fort D. A. Russell to establish order in the town.

The Indians were most active through Nebraska and Wyoming. In one Indian attack on a Mormon grading crew, two men were killed, the first men to be buried in the cemetery at Cheyenne. Another Indian attack led to the discovery of the pass called Sherman Hill. General Dodge himself was with the crew when the Indians set upon them. The railroad men escaped over a ridge, which General Dodge named for his old commander in the Civil War. Later he discovered that this hill was the easiest route over the Continental Divide.

Chief Spotted Tail of the Sioux once tried to scare a crew into giving him and his warriors a load of supplies. The crew foreman was not scared, and the chief had to leave empty-handed. A later attempted raid ended disastrously for the Indians. It was near Fort Wallace in Kansas. The red men had stretched a rawhide rope across the tracks to stop the train. The ends of this rope were held by painted warriors, fifty on each side of the rails. When the engine hit the stretched rawhide, it did not stop but sent the Indians flying through the air. Several were killed, and others were seriously wounded. They never tried that particular trick again.

By the middle of 1868 the Central Pacific had conquered the

Here Central Pacific crews are shown laying track and telegraph lines across Nevada in 1868. *Southern Pacific Company*

The Continental Divide marked the highest point that had to be crossed by the Union Pacific rails. *Deseret News*

A stretch of the first tracks laid across Wyoming. *Union Pacific Railroad Museum Collection*

9

SO MUCH LAND TO FILL

The completion of the first transcontinental line focused the attention of the whole country on the Pacific coast. Now that the Rockies and the Sierras and the plains and deserts and rivers of the continent had been mastered, many a railroad company looked to the Far West, and the word "Pacific" crept into their names. Among these were the Chicago, Rock Island and Pacific, the Missouri Pacific, the Northern Pacific, the Southern Pacific, and the Texas and Pacific, in addition to the two firsts — the Union Pacific and the Central Pacific.

This was not strange. More than half the United States lies west of the Missouri River. The region was largely uninhabited. Millions of acres of land for farming, cattle raising, timbering, and mining lay there waiting for the hands and machines of settlers to make use of them for the benefit of the entire country. It was up to the railroads to supply men and equipment for this wide, empty territory.

Under the Pacific Railroad Act of 1862, one great drawback to an extensive system of railroads had been eliminated. This was the wide diversity of gauges in use. As was shown in Chapter 5, at first each railroad decided on the gauge it would use, so there was no uniformity. This was often done on purpose so that the locomotives of one line could not use the tracks of a competitor. But now that trains were to run from New York City to San Francisco, using several different lines, it was seen that a uniform gauge was necessary.

This act gave the President the right to decide on the gauge for the transcontinental lines. President Lincoln wanted a 5-foot gauge, but Congress set the 4-foot 8½-inch gauge, which was gradually accepted by most companies. This gave a great impetus to railroad building and to travel.

A year after the ceremony at Promontory, a delegation of 100 people traveled from Boston to San Francisco in six days, without changing cars. This was the longest journey, up to that time, made

This shows an early Union Pacific dining car, crowded with portly men and a few women. The little girl was unusual enough to warrant giving her special attention. *Union Pacific Railroad*

This shows one of the special trains that crossed the continent in the 1870's. It was the famous Jarrett and Palmer special train, which made the run from New York to San Francisco in eighty-four hours and seventeen minutes. The fastest regular passenger service was seven days. *Southern Pacific Company*

anywhere in the world over continuous railroad tracks. It was also the fastest long journey made by man. It captured the imagination of the whole country and set people agog to see far places.

On this journey great changes in railroad travel were apparent. The cars were large and comfortable, paneled in gleaming wood with brass and nickel trim. Tapestry and plush upholstered the wide seats. Plate-glass windows let in the sunlight by day, and gas jets lighted the cars at night. Meals were served in an elegant dining car, with tables covered by damask cloths and furnished with silver, crystal, and fine china. Sleeping berths were convenient and comfortable; lavatories and toilets for men and women were elegantly furnished. There was a barbershop, a bathroom, a music room, and a library. This train even carried a printing establishment from which was issued a daily four-page newspaper.

This was the first of a long list of special trains which were to increase their rich appointments, year after year, as they vied for elegance. But not yet were all trains, or even the majority of them, so ornate. Still, all over the country, as soon as the Civil War ended, new railroad companies were formed to take advantage of the interest in Western travel.

About the time that the Central Pacific began constructing its road, a man named Cyrus K. Holliday received from Congress a grant of 3,000,000 acres of land in Kansas. This was to help him build a railroad that would enable the Southern states to reach the Pacific coast. Construction of this railroad, the Atchison, Topeka and Santa Fe, was delayed by various troubles — financial, political, and administrative. Construction actually began in the fall of 1868. The next year the company acquired its first train — a secondhand locomotive, an old day coach, twelve freight cars, and one handcar. This start would eventually develop into one of the great transcontinental systems, reaching from Galveston, Texas, to Chicago, Denver, and San Francisco.

Its particular job in building the country lay in its development of the cattle industry of the Southwest. Along its line sprang up towns, many of them almost strictly cow towns, known for the cowboys and the herds of longhorns from Texas that came to meet and use the trains. Dodge City, Queen of Cow Towns, was laid out in 1872, and in September of that year the first passenger train arrived, loaded with settlers, buffalo hunters, gamblers, and adventurers. At first, buffalo hunting was the main activity. Before the depot was built, buffalo hides were stacked high, awaiting shipment to the East. Within three years 25,000,000 or more of the great, shaggy animals had been slaughtered. A traveler said that at one time a person could walk for miles on the carcasses of the slain buffalo. Later the bones were collected and shipped for fertilizer. People said jokingly that in Dodge City buffalo bones were used for money.

Later came the great herds of Texas longhorns and the wild deeds of the cowboys. Luke Short, Wyatt Earp, and Bat Masterson strode along its board sidewalks, ostensibly trying to keep peace but probably adding their bit to the general roistering. Then, when the cattle days were over, the town became the center of a great wheat-raising region. Again, the railroad was important in shipping the grain to Eastern markets.

Farther north than the first transcontinental, another railroad was heading West. This was the Great Northern, the darling of James Jerome Hill.

Jim Hill has been called many things: the little giant, the empire builder, the man who made the West, and the man who wrecked the West. He is a hero to some, a villain to others, but he is important in any story of American railroads.

As a child playing Indian with other boys, Jim Hill was struck by an arrow, which cost him the sight of one eye. But it did not hinder his activity. In 1856 Jim left his home in Ontario, Canada, and ventured down to Pig's Eye, Minnesota, which was soon to change its name to St. Paul. The young man got a job on the waterfront, where he watched packet boats carrying Minnesota grain down the Mississippi to the cities below.

The river traffic was not the only transportation activity in the city. A short-line railroad was also doing business, but not very profitably. Young Hill decided that if he could buy up the little railroad, he could turn it into a moneymaking venture. Emigrants were streaming into Minnesota, particularly from Sweden. They were good, dependable farmers. The region was sure to prosper. So, with three companions, Hill purchased the line and began to extend it westward.

Railroad building was not easy up there in the north. There

The deep snows of the northern plains made it necessary to develop an efficient method of clearing the tracks of drifts. The rotary snowplow was invented and did a good job. *Union Pacific Railroad*

were dreadful blizzards in winter and dreadful droughts in summer. There were bands of hostile Indians and swarms of hungry grasshoppers. But Jim Hill kept his crews working in spite of difficulties, and he worked right along with them. There are many stories about Jim Hill. One tells how, in a blizzard, he took the pick from a shivering workman and sent the fellow to his own luxurious private car for coffee, while he, the president of the company, wielded the pick in the snow. Another shows a different side of the man. When a small-town mayor objected to the engines running through the streets at night, Hill tore down the station and moved it two miles out of the city. After that, the people of the town had to get to and from the depot as best they could.

The energy and driving force of this empire builder achieved one of the great railroad-building feats of all time. In seven and a half months his 8,000 workmen laid rails across the plains from Gassman Coulee, North Dakota, to Helena, Montana, a distance of 643 miles.

Crossing the Missouri River was another great feat. It was said that the most uncertain things in creation were "the action of a jury, the state of a woman's mind, and the condition of the Missouri River." In winter, rails were laid on the solid ice. In spring, the ice broke, floods came, and the tracks were washed away. But Hill's Great Northern bridged the river and went on north to the Canadian border, where it met the Canadian Pacific, down from Winnipeg.

Hill's only rival in the Northwest was the Northern Pacific, which was built from 1871 to 1881. It ran into trouble in 1893 and was bought by Hill. Now his competitor was part of his company, adding to his profits. But his own railroad had made a fortune. His name of empire builder had been well earned. He had taken a page from the Illinois Central's book and had sent agents to Norway and Sweden to sing the praises of the great Northwest. In this wide-open country a man could homestead a farm, getting land for nothing but his efforts. Or he could buy some of Hill's land for $2.50 an acre. Towns sprang up; bonanza farms spread across the land. These farms were so named because of their fabulous yields of wheat and their great size. Some were two or three townships in extent. They filled Hill's freight cars with grain to be carried to Puget Sound and from there in ships to Russia and the Orient. The returning ships brought the luxurious products of those exotic lands to enrich the lives of the settlers.

Hill did more for the region than just bring in settlers. To make sure that it prospered, he brought in fine blooded cattle to compete with the shipments from Texas. He gave away, free, millions of bushels of the finest grain for seed to the farmers on "his" lands. He started agricultural fairs, which gave his trains hundreds of passengers to and from the cities where the fairs were held. Later, his lines were sent east to Chicago and St. Louis. Now his trains could carry not only grain and cattle from the farms of Minnesota and North Dakota, but also lumber from Oregon; cotton from the South; meat from Omaha and Chicago; and copper from Montana.

James J. Hill's methods have been criticized as being ruthless and even underhanded. In some cases they were both. But his railroads were a tremendous help in building the Northwest. In later years, when the blizzards and droughts devastated the region, many settlers gave up and moved away. But the empire which Hill's railroads helped build is still a vigorous and vital part of the country.

The Atchison, Topeka and Santa Fe served the cattle and farm region, but there were cities and land farther south that could not sit idly by while the rest of the country prospered with railroads. As early as 1850 a group of men met in New Orleans to plan a way to share the good times brought by the steam cars. Colonel James E. Gibbs was the moving force behind this meeting, where plans were discussed and the decision made to build a railroad westward. The first goal would be Texas. After that, perhaps Mexico, perhaps the Pacific.

A company was formed and a charter obtained to build the New Orleans, Opelousas and Great Western Railroad, generally called simply the Opelousas. Colonel Gibbs was made chief engineer, with G. W. B. Bayley as his assistant. Work began in the spring of 1852; the first 80 miles took the rails to the Atchafalaya River.

At about the same time that the New Orleans group was meeting, several Texas businessmen purchased the right-of-way and the assets of a company that had been incorporated as far back as 1841 but had done nothing except a little grading of the roadbed for a railroad it planned to construct out of Harrisburg, Texas. The new group obtained a charter for the Buffalo Bayou, Brazos and Colorado Railroad. The moving spirits behind the new venture were General Sidney Sherman and William Rice. The line began at Harrisburg (now a part of Houston) and by 1855 had reached the Brazos, 30 miles to the west.

Out in California, railroads were being built hither and thither, from city to city. Most of these were short lines; all wanted to get to San Francisco so they could reap revenue from the goods brought by ship from the Orient. The Big Four of the Central Pacific were keeping an eye on all such projects and buying up any that threatened their own line. In this way the quartet acquired a line which was only in the planning stage — not a rail laid. It was called the Southern Pacific. It was planned to take this line south from San Francisco to San Diego and then to turn toward the East.

The finagling that went on, the buying and selling, the switching of names and routes, and the deals between companies are too complicated to go into here. It is enough to say that finally the Southern Pacific became the name of a great transcontinental line that crossed southern Arizona and Texas to New Orleans. In this eastward push it swallowed up both the New Orleans and the Texas lines. The Southern Pacific also went south from Yuma, Arizona, to Guadalajara, Mexico, under the name of the West Coast of Mexico Route. It went north from San Francisco to Portland, Oregon as the Shasta Route. And it went north from Houston to St. Louis as the Cotton Belt Route. And there were numerous branches, forming a great network that would serve the entire southernmost section of the country from the Mississippi to the Pacific.

To the Southern Pacific and the other lines into California must go the credit for the astounding growth of that state. First of all, the railroads started a rate war. First-class fare from Chicago to San Francisco in 1869 had been $130. By 1887 the SP was carrying passengers first class for $50. For a time the Santa Fe outbid all others and let settlers travel from Missouri to California for only $1.

Scores of zulu trains were put on the rails to make it easy for whole families to move to the coast. On these trains one member of the family would ride in the baggage or stock car to look after the household goods or animals. The rest of the family traveled in the passenger cars. The Southern Pacific alone poured 120,000 settlers into Los Angeles in a single year. Some of these went out into the country to establish farms or small towns, but at least a third remained in the city. Land prices boomed and fell. One unhappy speculator grumbled that he had lost $1,000,000, "And the worst thing about it was that $500 was in cash!" But the people still flocked to the Golden State, and most remained there.

In about twenty years after the laying of the last rail at Promontory, the trains were shuttling back and forth across the continent. Cities were springing up where only villages had been or where there had been nothing at all before the rails came. Undreamed-of resources in gold and silver and copper and oil, in farms that raised oranges and lemons and green vegetables all the year around, were being developed. New industries were springing up, and the whole character of the country was changing. This could not have happened with only wagon or river transportation. The railroad brought about this growth. There was much land to be utilized! Speed and ease of transportation were needed. No wonder people sang:

Yes, the Iron Horse is coming, and that's good news!
It will cure hard times and drive away the blues.
Ring your bells of welcome! Let the cheering resound!
Our wealth will come forth, for our wealth is in the ground.
And joy will kindle in the good farmer's eye
When he can buy so cheap and can sell his stuff so high!

10

SMALL LINES DO SPECIAL JOBS

The great railway systems spanning the continent were not the only lines helping build the country. Everywhere — north, south, east, and west — small individual lines were being constructed to do special jobs of transportation. Some of these were bought up by larger concerns, as were the Opelousas and the Buffalo Bayou. Some entirely disappeared. But others, whether operating now or not, achieved a fame which merits their inclusion in this book.

Some were the narrow gauges, or baby trains, as they were fondly called. While the war of the gauges was going on, some railroad builders refused to be told how to lay their tracks. A narrow gauge of 2 feet, 2½ feet, or 3 feet was more economical to build and run than a wider gauge. It used shorter ties and lighter rails and locomotives. And in some terrain there was scarcely room for the wider gauges. By 1876 there were 81 of these "little fellers" operating in twenty-six states. Most of these have disappeared, but where one still runs, it is an object of admiration by railroad buffs. Interested people travel for miles just to ride a narrow gauge; parents take their children on a holiday trip to let them have the thrill of this experience. A popular baby train is operated by the Denver and Rio Grande Western each summer, from May till October. The train makes one trip a day from Durango to Silverton and back. The fare is $6.50 for adults and $4.50 for children. People come from all parts of the West to make this 45-mile trip in the old-fashioned cars.

Colorado once had many miles of narrow-gauge railroad serving the mines and boomtowns of the Rockies. It was said that a narrow gauge could "curve on the brim of a sombrero," and sometimes, in those mountains, it had to do almost just that. But at first, even the trunk lines of the Denver and Rio Grande were laid in the 3-foot width. These have since been converted to the standard gauge, save for the one section mentioned.

A tiny train, almost a miniature, runs on the narrow **gauge** at the restored old mining town of Calico, California. *Knotts Berry Farm*

The narrow-gauge railroad still run each summer by the Denver and Rio Grande Western is seen on its way from Durango to Silverton, Colorado. *Denver and Rio Grande Western Railroad*

The people of Denver had been very disappointed when the Union Pacific went through Cheyenne, missing the Colorado capital by 100 miles. The Kansas and Pacific had started toward Denver right after the Civil War, but it had bogged down on the plains. It soon became evident that Colorado would have to build its own railroads.

General William Jackson Palmer had an idea that a railroad could be built south from Denver along the base of the Rockies, through Raton Pass in New Mexico and on to Mexico City. He believed that such a line would do much to build up that section of the country and that along this line great industrial cities would soon rise. Factories could use the coal from the mines at Trinidad, Colorado; machines would be fed by the agricultural products of the region. This railroad of General Palmer's scheme was also to go west to Salt Lake City and on to the Pacific coast.

Palmer chose the narrow gauge of 3 feet. Edward Gillette was

The Emma Sweeney, a 38-ton ten-wheel locomotive which operated for years on the narrow-gauge lines to the mining towns of Colorado. *Association of American Railroads*

A freight train on one of Colorado's narrow-gauge lines is making its way to Leadville. Old 76, pictured here, was the last narrow-gauge train operated by the Burlington Lines. The cars in the background are occupied by section crews converting the line to standard gauge. *Burlington Lines*

employed as chief engineer. Branches from the main line were to climb the steep slopes to the mines to bring down the wealth of the Rockies. Thus the Denver and Rio Grande, as the line was named, would do a double service in building the West.

The construction of this railroad was accompanied by some exciting events. In the summer of 1875 an epic battle took place between this line and its rival, the Atchison, Topeka and Santa Fe. The D and RG rails were to follow the bed of the Royal Gorge, sometimes called the Grand Canyon of the Arkansas. John C. Frémont had looked at this stupendous cleft and had declared it impassable by rail. But the D and RG planned to lay rails up this impossible route to the mining town of Leadville, perched high above the canyon floor.

The company had reached Canon City, a few miles east of the gorge, and had stopped there for a breather. The Santa Fe, also hoping for the business of the rich Colorado mines, was at Pueblo, about 40 miles southeast of Canon City. The Santa Fe officials thought they saw their chance. They knew the gorge was so narrow only one right-of-way was possible. If they sneaked a crew into the canyon and started to grade a roadbed, they would have that right-of-way cornered. A party of workers started by wagon from Pueblo.

The D and RG people were not asleep. They learned what was up and sent their own crew posthaste toward the mouth of the canyon. It was an exciting race, won by the D and RG men who reached the goal a bare half hour before their rivals. When the Santa Fe crew arrived, they found their competitors already busy on the road.

It did not end there. The two camps were determined to own this particular stretch. Guns were brought into play. Tracks laid by one crew during the day were torn up by the others during the night. It seemed to be a standoff, until finally a compromise was reached, and the D and RG was awarded the prize.

It was a bargain, even at the cost of the fight, which was estimated at $500,000. Even so, most people believed the tracks could never be laid. The canyon walls rose straight from the bedrock in sheer precipices. There was no place at all for a foothold for workmen. Men had to be lowered by ropes down over the cliff face to bore the holes into which dynamite could be placed. At one point the canyon was so narrow and the walls so perpendicular that no ledge could be carved there for the rails. So a hanging bridge was suspended from steel trusses driven into the granite walls. Over this swinging structure the little engines puffed their way. Later a heavier, stronger bridge replaced this first structure.

Many tales are told of how the baby trains proved to be heroes of the mountain slopes. They had to combat not only steep grades and sharp curves, but also winter blizzards and springtime floods. The head of steam would be exhausted by some difficult climb, and the tiny locomotives would have to stop, panting like tired animals, until it could be built up again. Once a circus train from South Park, heavily loaded with animals and equipment, could not make the final grade into Leadville. For a few moments there was consternation. The troupe thought it could not reach the town in time for the advertised show. Then the head animal trainer had an idea. He brought out three big elephants, maneuvered them into position with their heads against the rear coach, and shouted his commands. The elephants pushed, and the train began to move. So, with elephant power in place of steam, the little locomotive drew its cars into town.

From its exciting beginning, the Denver and Rio Grande went on to become one of the great lines serving the West. Today it is known as the Denver and Rio Grande Western Railroad.

A notable name in the story of Colorado's narrow-gauge railroads is that of Otto Mears, a Russian-born immigrant. Brought to

California by his parents when he was thirteen, Mears was soon left an orphan. He began to peddle notions in the mining towns of the Mother Lode, finally drifting east to Colorado. He settled down in the Conejos Valley in the southern part of the territory.

A trader at heart, the ex-soldier (he had served in the Civil War) decided there would be sizable profits in building roads to the isolated mining camps. He set to work first constructing wagon roads and later laying tracks for trains. His most spectacular feat was building the road over the Red Mountain. Today this route is followed by the Million Dollar Highway, one of the most scenic roads in Colorado or the West. On a section of one of Mears' roads, the stretch from Durango to Ridgeway, the train traveled 60 miles to cover what would be 25 miles in a straight line. It is over part of this road that the Denver and Rio Grande Western still operates the summer excursions of its narrow-gauge line.

Mears built some sections of the Denver and Rio Grande Southern Railroad and later became the president of this company. He became very rich and gave generously to the fund for erecting the State Capitol in Denver. His portrait in stained glass decorates a window in the dome of this building. Mears died in California in 1831, a seldom-recognized railroad builder.

Brigham Young and the Mormons in Salt Lake City, like the people of Denver, were disappointed when the Union Pacific rails bypassed them, going through Ogden instead of Salt Lake City. People in the East thought the Mormons wanted to be isolated from the rest of the country. They were surprised at the eagerness with which the Utah people awaited the coming of trains, singing:

> The great Pacific Railway,
> For California, hail!

Bring on the locomotive!
Lay down the iron rail!

Eliza R. Snow, the Mormon poet, wrote:

Haste, O haste, construct a Railway
    Where the vales of Ephraim bloom;
Cast ye up, cast up a highway
    Where "swift messengers" will come: . . .

And we soon shall hail as neighbors
    Those who dwell in lands afar,
As they move across the sage-plains
    On the swiftly-gliding car!

This painting by Utah artist Maynard Dixon depicts Brigham Young giving instructions to a crew of railroad workers.

This photograph of the first train to enter Salt Lake City was taken on the morning of January 10, 1870. It was on its way from Ogden to Salt Lake City, over Brigham Young's Utah Central Railroad.

When the rails bypassed the capital of Utah Territory, Brigham Young wasted no time. He set his Mormon boys to work building branch lines. These husky young men worked with a will, singing:

Hurray! Hurray! The Railroad's begun!
Three cheers for our contractor, his name's Brigham Young!
Hurray! Hurray! We're light-hearted and gay,
Just the right kind of boys to build a railway!

Within a year the Utah Central Railway from Salt Lake City to Ogden had been completed to make it possible for Utahans south of Ogden to make use of the transcontinental line. Then various lines were built to the southern parts of the territory and northward from Ogden to Logan and to Silver Bow, Montana. All the valleys of the territory were now served by railroads, but the mountainous regions

A bridge in Echo Canyon, Utah, with a tunnel in the background. Rails through the canyon were first laid by Mormon workmen.

daunted the Utahans. For years there would have to be slow wagon travel to the railheads at Corinne or Modena or Logan. However, as mines opened in Utah, railroads were built to such towns as Park City in the Wasatch Mountains.

In Nevada, too, the mines were responsible for the construction of special railroads. One of these, the Virginia and Truckee, achieved a certain fame of its own. Measured in terms of the rich loads it carried, this little line was once the richest railroad in the world. Almost its only freight was the fabulous ores from the Comstock that it carried down to the mills on Carson River. Its passengers were generally rich mineowners and mine operators in striped trousers, frock coats, and tall silk hats. Their bearded faces and watch-chain-decorated paunches indicated the opulent lives they enjoyed.

The region was still a part of Utah Territory when four Irish prospectors discovered what came to be known as the Comstock

Lode, one of the richest bonanzas in the history of mining. By the end of the Civil War the surface outcroppings had been worked out, and it looked as if the Comstock were finished. On the slopes lay piles of slag containing millions of dollars' worth of silver, left there because it would not pay to haul the slag by wagon to the mills. No one seemed to know that more silver lay deeper underground.

No one, that is, save a Virginia City lawyer named William Sharon. This dapper little man decided that what the Comstock needed was a railroad. He went down to San Francisco and interested some bankers in his scheme. All that would have to be done, he said, was to lay rails from Virginia City to Carson City. Then the low-grade ores could be shipped economically and profitably to the mills. On the return trips the cars could carry lumber, equipment, and supplies. The bankers were interested, and work began:

During the 1870's the J. W. Bowker hauled millions of dollars' worth of gold from the Comstock to Reno, Nevada. *Gulf Oil Company*

At first it was planned to make the little line only 15 miles long — just down to the mills on Carson River — or, perhaps, a few miles longer, into Carson City itself. But the Central Pacific by this time was laying its rails through Reno. It was decided that it would be wise to make the line still longer, to meet the transcontinental line.

Chinese workmen, who had gained experience on the Central Pacific, were engaged to grade the roadbed. Henry M. Yerrington was general superintendent. He was later honored by having the town of Pizen Springs renamed for him. On September 28, 1869, Yerrington drove a silver spike into the first rail laid in the new line.

The construction was followed with intense interest by everyone in the region. It became popular to take picnic lunches out to the site and to enjoy the meal while watching the laborers. Special excursion trains ran as far as the tracks were laid, girls in summer frocks and men in round straw hats crowding from cowcatcher to caboose. Never was another railroad built with so much jollity and noise.

Three engines were ordered from the East. They came dismantled and were hauled into Virginia City by wagon. Two Baldwin locomotives, came ready to go, but they had to be drawn by eighteen yoke of sweating oxen across the Truckee meadows from Reno.

The little Lion, one of the knocked-down locomotives, was assembled first, and to it went the honor of drawing the first train of cars from Virginia City over the high wooden trestle into Goldfield. There its welcome outshone the celebration at Dunkirk, New York, when the Erie Railroad was completed.

The Virginia and Truckee line was destined to set the style in luxurious train accommodations. The plain long coaches of the early trains soon became elegant cars with plush-upholstered seats. Smoking cars, ornate dining cars, and observation coaches were added to meet the demands of the wealthy passengers. George M. Pullman himself rode in one of his own fine sleepers from Reno to Virginia City to prove that these elegant cars could make the grade to the mountain city. Other noted passengers would be President Ulysses S. Grant, General William Tecumseh Sherman, the rich Baron Rothschild, and Leland Stanford, governor of California. The governor's private car, costing $30,000, had been given to him by his wife. Actors, singers, dancers, and whole circuses rolled gently up the slopes to perform in Piper's Opera House in Virginia City.

The Virginia and Truckee had a real job to do in the development of the West — the job of transporting ores from the Comstock to the mills. This it did faithfully and well. But it also did something else. It brought in wealthy and talented people to give the lonely miners a taste of elegance. It turned the isolated mountain-mining community of Virginia City into a center of culture and social life.

Far across the continent, in Florida, the "railroad that went to sea" is an interesting example of how a small, independent line was instrumental in developing a region. To Florida's East Coast Railway that state owes much of its present prosperity, including such rich and flourishing cities as Miami and Palm Beach. Henry Flagler, who built the line, was not, like Otto Mears, a poor man seeking a way to make money. He was already a fifty-three-year-old millionaire when he went to Florida in the 1880's.

At the old town of St. Augustine, said to be the oldest city established by Europeans on the continent of North America, the rich visitor found no accommodations to suit his taste. Flagler decided to remedy this situation, for he felt that with adequate facilities Florida could attract many wealthy vacationers. But to build a hotel, he would have to bring in men, equipment, and supplies. So he purchased the small Jacksonville-St. Augustine railroad. Then he went to work to erect the elaborate Ponce de Leon Hotel.

This was the first of a series of such hotels Flagler would build from St. Augustine to Key West, the southernmost city of the continental United States. Line by line, Flagler bought up various small railroads, which he merged into his Florida East Coast Railway. By 1896 he had a continuous line from Jacksonville to Miami — 366 miles. But there was no Miami before Flagler came. His engineers at St. Augustine, bent over their drawing boards, laid out this fabulous city. Then Flagler's railroad nursed it into becoming the great holiday metropolis it is today.

The builder was not content to stop here. He envisioned a line to Key West and perhaps beyond this, to Cuba. He set to work to build his dream into reality. It was a fabulous undertaking. At first, Flagler and his chief engineer, Tom Campbell, planned to lay the rails right through the Everglades. This mysterious and scarcely known region was expected to attract many visitors. But the survey of that area showed that such a line would be impossible. Reluctantly, Henry Flagler decided to lay his route across just a corner of the Everglades, avoiding the swampy, mosquito- and alligator-infested interior. From the Everglades the road would leap from island to island to its goal.

Flagler had more than a flamboyant idea in mind. He wanted to set up a route that would enable the ships from South America to unload their cargoes much sooner than they were doing. Trains could then carry the freight up to the Eastern centers in far less time than the ships could make the trip. In this way, he could capture much of the South American trade. Moreover, rail connection with Cuba would bring the tobacco from that island of the West Indies to Key

140

West in record time. Key West was then the world's largest cigar-manufacturing center. Flagler thought his railroad would be of value to this whole far Southern region, as well as profitable to himself.

At least thirty small islands lay between the Florida coast and Key West. (The word "key" is from the Spanish *cayo*, meaning a low island or reef.) From island to island went the surveyors, growing every day more sure that the plan was impossible. Between some keys the water was so shallow a causeway could be made by filling in with rock and earth. Between others a bridge would have to be built. Some of these bridges would have to be many miles long. In places the current was so deep and swift it would be almost impossible for such work to be carried on there. Added to all these difficulties were tropical storms, even hurricanes, fires, and insects to battle.

Henry Flagler and Tom Campbell went ahead. They encoun-

The Havana Special on Flagler's Long Key, Florida, viaduct. This oversea extension was abandoned in 1935 after a severe hurricane. *Florida East Coast Railway*

The Oregon Pony, the first railroad engine used in the Pacific Northwest, hauled lumber worth millions from the forests of Oregon. *Union Pacific Railroad*

tered every sort of difficulty, including labor problems and accidents to the workers. But bit by bit they constructed the roadbed and laid the rails. On January 22, 1912, the Extension Special from Miami to Key West flashed into the terminal at that southernmost city. It was welcomed as other triumphant trains had been welcomed, with cheers and bands and flying flags. "Flagler's Folly" had become the eighth wonder of the world.

The "railroad that went to sea" had cost nearly $30,000,000, but it was a boon to Key West. During the year or two after its completion, the population soared to 22,000. From Key West to Cuba the trains were taken on ferries, extending the railroad service 90 miles farther. This road operated for less than twenty-five years. In 1935 a hurricane destroyed much of the railroad and the equipment. Whether the loss of the railroad was the cause or not, the prosperity of Key West was doomed. Once judged the richest city per capita in the country, it was soon bankrupt. But Flagler's railroad had laid a roadbed over much of which a new concrete automobile highway would be laid. It had given birth to Miami and Palm Beach and had stimulated the growth of Jacksonville, St. Augustine, Daytona Beach, and other cities along its route.

The railroads chosen for examples of how smaller lines served the country are typical of many, many railroads from Oregon to Oklahoma, from Vermont to Florida. Their work is often forgotten in admiration of the great deeds of the trunk lines. But here and there in the history of some location is found a story that points up the romance of the little fellers — the short lines, the narrow gauges, and the short-lived independent roads.

11

TWO SPECIAL GIFTS

In addition to all their other services, the railroads have given the country two special gifts: One of these has done much to regulate our entire lives; the other has changed the landscape. The first is standard time; the second is the railroad station.

It is difficult today to imagine how mixed up the country once was in the matter of time. Every large city and every region had its own time. The workday was not from a definite morning hour to a definite afternoon hour; it was from sunup to sundown. People were not very careful about the exact hour, much less the minute, of an appointment or a stagecoach's arrival or departure. Coaches and trains, for a long time, ran on rather indefinite schedules. The nearest hour was posted, but since arrivals were often very late, it was not uncommon for people to wait long hours at stations. This system had seemed to work fairly well for stagecoaches and canalboats, which traveled rather slowly. When trains began to move at 20, 30, and even 60 and 70 miles an hour, it was a very different matter. Not only the hour, but the exact minute of arrival and departure, had to be known.

Each railroad company adopted its own time. This caused great confusion, especially in cities into which several lines came. In a city like Chicago, a number of clocks hung on the station walls, each showing the time of a particular railroad. No two clocks were alike. Six different lines ran into Pittsburgh, Pennsylvania, so in that station there were seven clocks, one for each railroad and one to show the local Pittsburgh time. Even within a single state there were many different times: Illinois had twenty-seven, Wisconsin, thirty-eight. A transcontinental traveler, who wished to keep the exact time on his watch, had to adjust the timepiece twenty times between the Atlantic and the Pacific. It was all very confusing.

It was the railroads that came to the rescue. On her summer trip

A conductor and an engineer compare watches. Fast-running trains must meet schedules on the exact minute. *Union Pacific Railroad Museum Collection*

to Niagara Falls in 1845, Miss Leslie had noted the inconvenience caused by the different times shown in the stations. She did not, of course, suggest a remedy. That was beyond her imagination. But she did think that something should be done.

Some twenty-five years later a more inventive advocate took up the problem. Professor C. F. Dowd, principal of a girls' school in Saratoga, New York, began to agitate for some sort of uniform time for the country. Since the globe-shaped earth is divided into 360 degrees, Professor Dowd suggested that it could also be divided into time zones. If each zone were 15 degrees wide, there would be exactly twenty-four. These could start at Greenwich, England, which is on 0 degrees of longitude, and proceed westward, in the direction the sun seems to move. (We know it only appears as if the sun moves; but it is the earth's rotation that causes day and night.)

Such a division of the earth's surface into time belts, or zones, would place four zones across the continental United States. Since there are twenty-four hours in a day and twenty-four time zones, each zone would represent one hour of time — that is, each zone would be figured as one hour earlier than the zone to the east and one hour later than the zone to the west. The four zones would be called Eastern, Central, Mountain, and Pacific. When it was 12 noon in Chicago, which would lie in the Central zone, it would be 1 P.M. in New York, 11 A.M. in Denver, Colorado, and 10 A.M. in San Francisco.

Professor Dowd wrote letters to Congress, to the railroad owners, and to the newspapers. He stirred up so much interest that in the spring of 1872 a number of railroad executives met in St. Louis to discuss the problem. They all knew that something must be done, because more and more people were traveling farther and farther. There had to be some uniformity in schedules to eliminate the inconvenience of long delays between trains, missed connections, and confused passengers. The railroad men discussed several solutions, but Professor Dowd's seemed best. They agreed to try it out. But it was to be eleven years — November 18, 1883 — before the plan was put into operation.

As with all changes, there were doubters. Many people felt it was tampering with nature to regulate one's activities by an artificial and arbitrary rule rather than by nature's own clock, the sun. The Minneapolis *Sentinel* declared, "The sun is no longer boss of the job. People, 55 million of them, must eat, sleep and work, as well as travel, by railroad time."

Thousands awaited the change with enthusiasm, and the change-over was accomplished without any real difficulty. Chicago was chosen as the key point, and when a telegraphic message indicated that it was exactly 12 noon in the center of the Central zone, all the railroad clocks in Chicago and throughout that zone were set at 12. At the same moment all the railroad clocks in the Eastern zone were set, or were expected to be set — some diehards refused to comply! — at 1 P.M.; those in the entire Mountain zone were set at 11 A.M.; and in the Pacific zone at 10 A.M. That was all there was to this momentous change in American life.

Because the railroads had by this time assumed so much importance, the entire country soon began to run on railroad time. This was not officially approved by Congress until nearly thirty-five years later. On March 19, 1918, Congress passed the Standard Time Act, making the zones official. During the years there have been some changes. In 1966 Congress adopted the Uniform Time Act, which established eight standard time zones for the United States, to include Alaska, Hawaii, and all U.S. possessions. Also, the act made provision for daylight saving time, whereby clocks are advanced one hour during the summer months. This gives more clock hours of daylight. People get up an hour earlier each day and so have an extra hour of light in the evening. Daylight saving, like all other changes, has had its opponents, and any state legislature can exempt its state from conforming.

On her trip across New York State, Miss Leslie found many things about the railroad stations — when there were stations — that needed improvement. No food was available, save at the town's hotel, which might be some distance from the railroad. Passengers were allowed only a few minutes to hurry to the hotel, grab a bite, and return. But some always dallied, annoying the prompt travelers and holding up the departure of the train.

The stations did not have their names set up plainly for the traveler to see. As a result, a person often rode right past the town he wished to visit and might be put off the train some miles past his destination.

Miss Leslie's complaints were valid, but she was fortunate to find any accommodations at all in 1845. Less critical travelers accepted the lack of conveniences without much complaint. In 1833, when the Charleston and Hamburg line in South Carolina was the longest railway track in the world, a New Englander took a ride on the Best Friend of Charleston just for the thrill of it. He later described the services found at Blackville, where an overnight stay was necessary.

The train had left Charleston at 8 A.M. and at 6:30 P.M. it stopped at Blackville, having traveled 90 miles that day. The village boasted only two or three log cabins and a half-finished tavern. There was no real depot, but a square, rough-boarded building stood beside the tracks. Here, in five jerry-built rooms, the twenty-five to thirty passengers had to spend the night. They warmed themselves by outdoor fires, then went inside for supper. The room was furnished with a few old chairs and a table. The supper was miserably cooked and sloppily served. The four "bedrooms" were a series of stall-like cubicles, with walls that reached only partway to the ceiling. Each cubicle held three or four beds. All the lady passengers were crammed into one cubicle, three to a bed. The men filled the other three. In the morning, breakfast was served. The food and lodging cost $4. In the tavern of the town, similar accommodations cost $1.50 per day.

Two years after this uncomfortable journey the first real railroad station in the world was built by the Baltimore and Ohio Railroad on Mont Clare Street, Baltimore. This was a substantial square structure of two stories. There was no platform to make it easier to board the train, but a short flight of stone steps led to the front door. Inside, there were hard wooden benches and a stove. It was from this depot that the first train for Washington would depart, but the country's capital had no real station at that time. Soon, however, one would be built — a narrow three-story frame building, with a low shedlike extension on each side.

As late as the 1870's as large and busy a city as New York had very poor accommodations for those arriving or departing on its trains. A sketch made at the time shows the terminal of the New York, Harlem and Albany Railroad, on Forty-second Street and Park Avenue. A wooden shed housed the ticket office, but there was no waiting room. The train came to a stop on a street deep in mud, littered with debris, and filled with rooting pigs and cackling hens. So much water filled the depressions that flocks of ducks were happily splashing about. Women had to lift their long, heavy skirts high to avoid the mud while small boys stomped their feet to make a big splash.

On this site, in 1871, Commodore Vanderbilt began construction of his Grand Central Terminal, which would stand for years as the greatest railroad station in the world, a sight to attract and dazzle the visitors to the city. The train shed was awe-inspiring: 600 feet long, 200 feet wide, and 100 feet high, with a curved glass roof above the twelve tracks. Gas jets in great chandeliers lighted the interior. To keep the big, beautiful room free of smoke, no engines were permitted to enter it. Instead, the engines were speeded up just before they came to the depot. Then, while still moving, they were uncoupled and run off onto a sidetrack. The cars coasted into the station under their own momentum.

With his Grand Central Terminal, Vanderbilt had a large new freight building constructed. It was of brick, with a bronze bas-relief decorating the front. This showed the whole history of transportation, from the most primitive beginnings through the Conestoga wagons, canalboats, and, finally, steam cars. His own figure towered over the panorama.

Cornelius Vanderbilt, whose Grand Central Terminal, built in New York in 1871, was the greatest railroad station in the world. *Association of American Railroads*

North front of the Great Central Railway Station at Chicago, opened in 1856 and used until 1892. Shortly after it was built, it was described as the largest and most magnificent railway depot in America. The first sleeping cars ever operated in the West ran out of this station. *Illinois Central Railroad*

During the next century the original depot was to be razed and rebuilt several times, always on the same site and always one of the great stations of the world. Today it is one of two great depots in the city, the other being the Pennsylvania Station, completed in 1910. It covers three city blocks and houses more than 100 tracks on its two levels. Some 45,000,000 passengers annually use 450 daily trains.

The Grand Central Terminal was a model for other large cities to copy and try to surpass. And so came into being the great age of depot building, during which some beautiful and some strange and wonderful structures were erected.

For almost 100 years, the railroad station was the main feature

151

Today's Union Pacific station at Boise, Idaho, resembles a California mission. *Union Pacific Railroad*

of most communities. Generally placed at the edge of the town, it was as grand and ornate as could be afforded. To most people, the station represented the status and worth of the community — not only of its wealth, but also of its moral and cultural ambitions. Turrets and towers, mansard roofs and gables, pillars and colonnades decorated the more pretentious buildings. The imagination of the architects ran riot.

The decoration varied as much as the architecture. Exteriors of brick or stone might be trimmed with statues, a bas-relief, or bronze plaques. Wooden buildings were painted in bright colors with contrasting trim. Inside the more ornate were fountains and statues, and murals and huge mosaics that depicted some historic event or personage. The more humble relied on paint and placards and advertisements to give color to the walls.

As the trains moved across the open spaces, with only small settlements at stops, the station became more utilitarian — a shelter from storms and heat, with wooden benches and a great stove. Around this stove, toward train time, the men of the town would gather to exchange their views on politics and industry. But as soon as the town warranted a better image of itself, a new station was erected, as elaborate and grand as could be afforded.

Many of the early railroad depots have disappeared or are standing vacant and unused. Others have been purchased and put to new

In the Far West the stations were utilitarian affairs that offered little save shelter to those who had to wait for a late train. *Union Pacific Railroad Museum Collection*

Men of the town liked to gather at the depot to exchange ideas while waiting for the train. This is the Rock Springs, Wyoming, station when diamond stacks were heading West. *Union Pacific Railroad Museum Collection*

use as homes, or shops, or restaurants, or something else far from their original purpose. For some years it has been quite the thing to convert an old station into a private home.

But for nearly 100 years the railroad station served the country well. To it would come the stages and wagons bringing travelers from outlying districts. There the travelers could wait and talk, sheltered and warm, until the train arrived. Often the first streetcar tracks in a city were laid from midtown to the depot.

As travel increased, more and more facilities for the comfort of the passengers were added. Providing for food was among the first of such improvements. Godey, like Miss Leslie, had been annoyed at not being able to purchase food at train stops. In a rather crotchety editorial he suggested that ham sandwiches be sold at stations. His idea was not adopted for some years, but food had to be supplied somehow. The "how" was the depot lunchroom, where murky coffee, stale sandwiches greasy doughnuts, and pie were offered. Usually the train stopped at some station in the morning and evening and about noon. This would be announced by the conductor as a meal stop. As soon as the wheels ceased turning, the hungry passengers would make a dive for the doors. No kindness or courtesy was shown the old, the women, or the children. It was each for himself.

In Kansas, in the 1870's, a man named Frederick H. Harvey was operating restaurants in small towns. When he took a journey by train and had to eat in one of the unpleasant depot lunchrooms, he got a brilliant idea. He took it to Charles F. Morse, the superintendent of the Santa Fe Railroad, which ran through the state. It was

A railroad station in the 1860's was a busy place with stagecoaches and carriages bringing passengers to the train and waiting for newcomers to take back to the city. *Association of American Railroads*

Often the first streetcar tracks in a city were laid to the depot. Here a mule car in Salt Lake City is on its way to the Denver and Rio Grande station. *Salt Lake City Lines*

an astounding idea: Harvey would set up a depot eating room that would be as clean and as attractive as any city hotel dining room. The service would be excellent, the food attractive and appetizing. Morse liked the idea and gave Harvey permission to try it out.

The first Harvey dining room was opened at the Topeka station. In a room clean and freshly painted, on tables covered with white cloths and furnished with linen napkins, good china and silver, Fred Harvey served his customers the best food he could buy, prepared by the best chefs he could hire. From the first meal, the project was a success.

Courtesy and decorum were insisted upon. Instead of grabbing food across a dirty counter, travelers sat down at a table and were served by neat, attractive waitresses. These soon became known as the Harvey Girls. They had to be "of good character, attractive and intelligent." So attractive and intelligent were they that they did not have to be employed long before most of them received proposals of marriage from the satisfied male customers. The girls wore a neat and modest uniform of black dress with white collar and black bow, a white apron, and black shoes and stockings. They were paid $17.50 a month, with board, and were allowed to keep their tips. To be a Harvey Girl from 1880 on was to have a pleasant and profitable job.

Fred Harvey's idea paid him well. Before he died in 1901, he and the railroad owned and operated fifteen hotels, forty-seven restaurants, and thirty dining cars. Harvey and his girls are credited with doing much to civilize the raw frontier. At least they did much to eliminate the uncouth happenings at the railway stations.

12

FOR MORE THAN PASSENGERS

Although the railroads have done an excellent job of moving people from place to place and of building up the country by transporting raw materials and manufactured products, they have, at the same time, performed many other necessary tasks. One of these has been the carrying of mail.

The Constitution gives Congress the right to establish post offices and post roads. It was well understood that so important a project as carrying the mail should be handled by the government. Still, for many years the mail was carried by private individuals or by companies formed for this purpose. Schedules were uncertain, rates variable, and communication with absent friends or relatives was precarious.

The British colonies had tried to remedy conditions by improving roads and carriers, but in 1773, when Benjamin Franklin was named colonial postmaster, it took two and a half days for a letter to go from New York to Philadelphia; there was one mail a week in summer and two a month in winter. Franklin reduced the time to 36 hours and increased the service to three times a week.

Still, the mail was carried by private individuals, on horseback or by stage, the letters stuffed into the crown of a high beaver hat or into the pockets of the messenger's coattails. As often as not, letters were simply entrusted to a traveler who had no responsibility, merely his goodwill.

After the United States was established, Congress tried to regulate mail service by selecting the men or companies to be awarded contracts for carrying letters and valuables over designated routes or post roads. Where no such roads existed, as into Ohio Territory, mail was sent by canal or river or stage over the shortest route to key centers. In 1795 the government was employing fifteen men and their boats at a cost of $4,000 a year to carry mail to the Ohio country.

Only seventeen years later John Stevens published a pamphlet on the advantages of a steam railway over canal transportation. In this — probably the first published work on railways — the inventor urged that the ownership and management of the country's railroads should be in the hands of the federal government. One of the important reasons for such ownership would be that trains could be used for transporting mail. Congress paid scant attention to the ideas presented.

However, the first regularly scheduled train service had not been in operation a year before it was carrying U.S. mail.

This was in South Carolina, where the Best Friend of Charleston was operating between Charleston and Hamburg, a distance of 136 miles. On a wintry day in November, 1831, the man who had the contract for transporting the mail between the two cities tossed a

159

locked pouch onto a railway car and sent it flying toward its destination. This was the first time U.S. mail was ever carried by rail.

As railway communication was established between more and more cities, the mail contractors naturally gave up traveling by horse or stage to use the faster service. But they still carried the letters and small packets in their hats or pockets or carpetbags. The volume of mail grew, and a locked pouch, then a trunk, was introduced. Finally, it was necessary to use an entire car — one that could be locked to protect the valuable contents it held. But by this time the great express companies had been formed. They still sent a guard, or messenger, along with the mail, but it was handled, not directly by the government, but by companies who held contracts from the government.

Congress had taken steps to make this possible. In July, 1838, it passed an act making every railroad in the country a post road. President Martin Van Buren signed the act, and it became immediately legal to send mail by rail.

Events in California were taking place at a rapid rate in the 1840's and 1850's and the government tried a variety of methods of establishing faster mail service to the Pacific. At last the firm of Russell, Majors and Waddell came up with the idea of a fast overland express that would carry mail to the coast in less time than any other service. This was the noted pony express, which ran from St. Joseph, Missouri, to San Francisco. Trains carried the mail from Eastern cities to St. Joseph, where it was picked up by the pony express riders. From there on, horsepower, rather than steam, transported the mail.

At this time, mail was sorted at the individual post offices and put into locked pouches, each labeled for its destination. The postmaster at the station where a pouch was deposited, was supposed to be the only person who had a key to the lock. This must not have been always true, for the *Deseret News* of Salt Lake City carried daily complaints that pouches had been opened and mail, especially newspapers and magazines, had been extracted.

Working as a clerk in the post office at St. Joseph was a man of imagination named W. A. Davis. His office was one of the points where mail was sorted. After the mail arrived over the Hannibal and St. Joseph road, there was a delay while it was sorted before the pony express rider could pick up his load and set out westward. Davis suggested to his superiors that this delay could be avoided if the mail were sorted on the train before it reached St. Joseph. He was given permission to try his plan. It worked, and for months this delay was eliminated.

With the completion of the transcontinental telegraph in 1861, the pony express was no longer needed and was discontinued in October of that year. The need for haste in sorting the mail at St. Joseph vanished, and Davis' plan was dropped. But the movement of mail was too slow, and the government sent the first assistant postmaster, Selah R. Hobbie, to England to find out what was being done there.

Hobbie learned that England used a mail catcher, — a sort of net hung out from a car so it could snare the mail pouches suspended from poles beside the track. In this way the mail was picked up without delay, but it was still carried to a central office for sorting. Hobbie thought the whole system was too expensive to be used here. So the government looked about for a substitute scheme.

One was offered by George Armstrong, the assistant postmaster at Chicago. He suggested that mail be sorted while the trains were moving, as had been done in Missouri, but not only on small lines, all over the country. Armstrong was told to make an experiment, which he did. He persuaded the Chicago and Northwestern Railroad to remodel several old cars into what he thought were suitable cars for the purpose. They had to have work shelves and supports for pouches.

The cars were provided, and in August, 1864, the trial run was made under Armstrong's eye, with experienced mail clerks doing the work. It was, of course, successful, in spite of the objections that had been raised. These objections had varied from complaints at the expense to silly protests that it would be impossible to handle mail in a moving car because the wind would scatter it all along the right-of-way.

However, this system saved so much time that it was rapidly put into use on nearly every railroad in the country. In 1867 the Chicago and Northwestern built the first car designed especially as a mail car. It was 40 feet long, with windows and deck lights. A semi-circular distribution desk was built at one end, with a table on which the pouches could be opened. There were pigeonholed letter cases

Here is a mail train, with a wooden device beside the track to hold the mail sack, which would be snatched off as the train flew by. *Library of Congress*

The Fast Mail leaving Grand Central Terminal, New York, in 1875. This is one of William H. Vanderbilt's specials, with cream-colored cars, which carried only U.S. mail and the mail clerks. *New York Central System*

and a storage room. There was also a chair, a stove, a woodbox, and an ice cooler for the comfort of the clerks.

As the service developed, changes were made in the mail car. Wooden racks for the pouches were added, then metal frames to hold them. At first the mail clerk just reached out and snatched suspended mail pouches as the train whizzed by. Later, a mail catcher was installed, making the catching of the mail pouch much more certain and much safer for the clerk. By 1869 the railway mail service was so efficient it was possible to send a letter and receive an answer, between any two post offices from New York to Buffalo, within twenty-four hours. That same year Armstrong was made the first general superintendent of the new service.

The first mail cars were just a part of a regular passenger train, but within five years the idea of a special mail train had developed. George S. Bangs had succeeded Armstrong as general superintendent of the system, and it was he who suggested that a special train, carrying nothing but mail, be run from New York to Chicago. The government liked the idea but did nothing about it. It was William H. Vanderbilt, son of the old Commodore, who finally built the first mail train, snagging this honor for his New York Central Railroad with the Fast Mail. The train could not be mistaken — its elegant cream-colored cars were emblazoned with the coat of arms of the United States. It ran between New York and Chicago on tracks cleared to let it thunder by. It covered the distance in twenty-four hours — about the same speed of trains 100 years later — a miracle for the time. Later the Pennsylvania Railroad added the Limited Mail to run between the same two cities.

The idea of a special train thundering along with letters and valuables for distant destinations caught the imagination of the people. Posters in vivid colors, stories, songs, and plays dramatized the exciting project.

The railway mail service was carried on, aside from the fast mail, by the trains that now made a network of communication all over the country. To avoid delays and stops to pick up mail, the pouch to be delivered was hung out of the car window on a long steel arm. The stationmaster would pluck it off as the train whizzed by. In the smallest communities the postmaster or postmistress would stand on the platform, holding up the sack of mail for the conductor to snatch as the car passed. In better-equipped stations, an arm held the outgoing pouch to be picked up by the extended steel arm from the car.

The mail car was generally placed next to the tender, where it became a veritable death trap when an accident occurred. The oil lamps that lighted the car might send jets of kerosene over the flimsy letters and papers, setting the entire car ablaze.

In time, however, many improvements were made, and the mail

car became very safe and comfortable and efficient. The first cars, each with a wooden chair and a sorting shelf, gave way to air-conditioned cars with fluorescent lighting; there were couches, lavatories, and other conveniences for the clerks.

For nearly 100 years this service operated efficiently, often going beyond the call of duty in some special emergency. After the great Chicago fire in 1871, the railroad postal service handled thousands of tons of food and clothing sent to the victims of that disaster. Jim Fisk, who had robbed many an investor in the Erie Railroad, became a hero to some sentimental people when he filled a car with supplies and sent it to Chicago.

When the news it was spread that the humble that night,
   Were starving to death, slow but sure,
Jim Fisk loaded up the Lightning Express
   To feed all the hungry and poor.

This Currier and Ives lithograph depicts two Lightning Express trains leaving a junction in New York State in 1863. Note the differences in smokestacks, cabs, and tenders. *Association of American Railroads*

Another development of the railways was the railway express, which grew to serve the entire country but was especially helpful to the West, with its gold and silver mines.

It was difficult enough, in the early days of the country, to be sure that an ordinary letter would reach its destination. The fate of anything valuable, such as money or jewelry, was far more doubtful. It was obvious that such valuables could not be trusted to any Tom, Dick, or Harry. Whoever carried such things must have a character and reputation that invited trust. This necessity gave rise to the express messenger — a man who could be depended on to deliver any package to the person to whom it was addressed.

It is not known who was the first messenger in Colonial times, but by the time railroads were operating between the main cities of the Atlantic coast, several small express companies were in business. The man given the credit of being the father of the express business in America was William F. Harnden of Massachusetts. His company was organized in 1839 to carry letters, valuables, and newspapers between New York City and Boston.

Because this was a service needed in all parts of the country, other express companies appeared in many areas. The term "express" had long been used by people to describe this sort of activity. Among the mountain men of the early West, to ride express was to carry a message as fast as one could to its destination. Many of these first small companies and their founders did not last long, and their names and work have been lost. Others survived and became important factors in the country's development.

One of these was Alvin Adams, a Vermonter, who established Adams and Company to carry express between Boston and Worcester, Massachusetts. Later he extended his service to New York and Philadelphia and employed a number of assistants. By 1845 he had purchased Harnden's and other small companies and had formed them into the Adams Express Company.

One of Harnden's agents was Henry Wells, who was in charge of the office in Albany, to which city Harnden's service had spread. Harnden's death had permitted Adams to gain that company, but Henry Wells did not go with the sale. He formed a company of his own, with a partner, to carry express from Albany to Buffalo.

The two companies, Adams' and Wells', began to grow with a surprising rapidity, one reason being, perhaps, that they carried letters for less than the United States postage. Naturally, people patronized them, and to such an extent that the government was forced to lower its rates to stay in the mail-carrying business. In 1845 the government dropped the rate from twenty-five cents to five cents for letters sent less than 500 miles, and to ten cents for any others except those to the Pacific coast. In 1848 the rate was dropped to three cents a letter for the entire country.

In 1850 three of the big companies acquired several smaller units and then merged to form the American Express Company. This was not a corporation, but an association in which every owner of the company's stock was liable for its debts. The articles of association held some strange provisions. One that could scarcely work today was that no shares could be sold to married women, infants, or irresponsible persons. Among the directors was William Fargo, who was to have much to do with the Western expansion of railway express. Alvin Adams was now alone against this giant company.

Two years after the formation of the American Express Company, Henry Wells and William Fargo organized Wells, Fargo and Company. They wanted to benefit from the rich harvest of profits to be reaped from the goldfields of California, but the other directors objected. More than $60,000,000 worth of gold had been shipped from the mines by steamship express south to Panama, across the Isthmus by mule team, and north by ship. And it was the Adams Express Company that was carrying the gold and getting rich. Henry Wells and William Fargo thought they could break the monopoly, and they did.

It was seventeen years before the transcontinental railroad bridged the continent. During those years American Express east of the Missouri built up friendly relations with the various lines it used for its service. West of the Missouri, Wells, Fargo and the Adams Company established stagecoach express service between mines and shipping centers, and as soon as trains were available, both companies used them. For trains were not only faster, but safer (for a time) than the stagecoaches that had become the target of the masked highwayman.

While American Express was performing a great service for Eastern cities, banks, and individuals, the two great Western companies were doing much to build the West. They brought all sorts of merchandise and supplies to the West and shipped the gold dust to

Wells, Fargo banks were so sturdily built that many survive to this day, though long unused. This one is at Silver Reef, Utah, once a bustling mining center, now a ghost town.

the East. The old idea that the express companies were to transport only letters and valuables had long ago disappeared. This probably happened back in the forties when a Buffalo restaurant owner asked Henry Wells if he could please bring some oysters from Albany so the Buffalo customers could feast on that popular food. It was a stunning request — oysters carried more than 250 miles by stagecoach! But Wells was equal to the task. He brought in the oysters at a good profit, and everyone was satisfied.

As the country grew, the three great express companies — American; Wells, Fargo; and Adams — flourished. They managed by hook or crook to get rid of any competitors, even those sponsored by the railways or the government. During this time critics complained of the monopolies. The government instituted investigations, scandals arose, but the companies continued to do a job no one else seemed capable of doing.

Then in 1913 the U.S. parcel post was established. People had been clamoring for the government to handle the type of package generally entrusted to the express companies. After the Parcel Post Act was passed, such packages, up to a certain size, could be sent by mail at a uniform and very low rate.

When the United States entered World War I in 1917, it took over the railroads and used the express cars for transporting its troops, matériel, and equipment. The next year it merged the existing express companies into the American Railway Express Company.

This company lasted for about ten years. Then the main railroads of the country, eighty-six of them, banded together to buy it and renamed it the Railway Express Agency. It operates today, using not only trains, but airplanes and ships. What had once been a service performed by men and mules had come to be one of the many duties of the railroads.

13

THE GOLDEN AGE OF STEAM

For about fifty years — from the early 1870's to the 1920's — the steam railroad ruled the nation. Twin ribbons of iron linked cities and towns, isolated sections, resorts, and scenic areas to the centers of population. The rails went everywhere, and everybody rode them. For business or pleasure, to work and to play, people climbed aboard the train.

By 1870 the fundamentals of railroad construction and use had been learned. Now all the energy of the owners was directed toward the utilization and refinement of the devices already on hand. The trains of 1920 would resemble those of 1870 only in name and in the fundamental principles of steam locomotion.

During this golden age of steam many improvements were made, such as the adoption of air brakes and automatic couplers. Roadbeds were made better. Heavier locomotives and cars gave travelers a faster, smoother ride. Besides, the public was becoming more demanding. People were generally richer and had more leisure. Those fifty years saw many panics and disasters, but on the whole the country was flourishing, in spite of the tremendous gap between those who owned mines and mills and factories and the overworked, underpaid laborers who served them. There was little or no government control of the way a man made his fortune, and during this period many great fortunes were made. On the other hand, labor was beginning to find a voice in labor unions and in some acts of Congress.

The mines of the West had poured their riches of gold and silver and copper into the country's treasure chest. And when the rich lodes had been worked out, around the turn of the century, a young man in Bingham, Utah, discovered a way to process low-grade ores. D. C. Jackling's method pumped new life into the mining industry, which, in turn, stimulated railroad activity. Oil had been discovered at Titusville, Pennsylvania, in 1859, and by 1870 it was changing many

A passenger locomotive of 1897. *Association of American Railroads*

A powerful freight engine of 1897. *Association of American Railroads*

aspects of American life. The inventions of the telephone, the electric light, and the automobile were opening up new avenues of progress. Although each of these gave rise to monopolies and exploitation of workers and although panics and strikes erupted in many sections, trains filled with excited travelers were still flying over shining rails.

Every year these trains became larger, more beautiful, and more luxurious.

Locomotives lost their diamond stacks, or funnels, or Dolly Vardens and replaced these old-fashioned smokestacks with a straight, tall stack which was gradually shortened to the modern style. The cowcatcher was improved. Bell and whistle and powerful headlight were added. A comfortable steel cab sheltered the engineer. By 1920 the passenger locomotive was a trim, efficient machine; the freight engine was a powerful black monster that could draw long trains of heavily loaded cars up the steepest grades, with only the puffs of steam betraying their effort.

Freight cars were as varied as the load they carried. The mail car, the wooden express car, baggage cars, grain cars, cattle cars, coal cars, ore cars — each was designed to serve best its particular purpose. Even the shapes were different: there were flatcars, box cars, gondola cars, tank cars, refrigerator cars. Country youngsters loved to watch a long freight go by, a moving picture-book telling of cargoes from all sorts of far places.

But it was the passenger car that came into its glory during these fifty years. There was never the vast difference between first and second class that is found, even today, in European trains. If a passenger chose to ride in the day coach, he still enjoyed plush-upholstered seats with headrest and footrest, iced drinking water, lavatories, plate-glass windows, electric lights, and steam heat. A small table could be set up between seats for the convenience of those who wished to eat their lunch at their seats or to write letters or play cards. Train

The luxurious dining car of Frank Leslie's excursion train was shown in this illustration from the account of the trip. *Frank Leslie's Weekly*

boys, or news butchers, went through the cars selling candy, sandwiches, newspapers, and magazines. At night the porter would rent a pillow for a few cents; the reclining seat back would be lowered, the footrest extended, and a fairly comfortable couch enjoyed.

Those who chose a Pullman car had somewhat more elegant seats, which formed a real bed at night. Above them an upper berth could be let down from its daytime position against the ceiling. Pillows, sheets, and blankets were provided.

The dining cars were elegantly appointed with linens, silver, and fine china. The waiters in crisp white coats and aprons were the epitome of courteous service. The food was excellent, and it was a real treat to have a meal on a dining car of any of the major lines.

The Pullman reached the pinnacle of ornate display in the private car of the wealthy. Railroad tycoons, oil magnates, mine-owners, and rich politicians did not care to travel with the general

Observing the Sabbath Day on a luxurious parlor car, with organ music, hymnbooks, and footstools. *Library of Congress*

The famous suspension bridge near Niagara Falls, which was a great attraction in the early days of excursion trains. Some went to Niagara Falls partly for the thrill of riding across this bridge. *Library of Congress*

public, so they had their own elegant cars built and furnished to suit their taste. There was no limit to the amount a millionaire would spend on such a car. Jay Gould's private car cost $50,000. Among the features of these gorgeous cars were such things as marble baths, plate-glass mirrors, wood-burning fireplaces, a pipe organ, master-pieces of art, and solid-gold light fixtures.

As has been said, everybody rode the trains — for business or for pleasure, to get to a job, to get to a resort, or to view the country. In Chapter 11 there was an account of a New Englander who went to South Carolina to take a trip on the Best Friend of Charleston, simply for the thrill of riding on the longest railway in the world. Many people took a ride on the train to Niagara Falls to enjoy the shivers caused by traveling over the suspension bridge. No sooner had the rails reached Niagara Falls than young married couples decided that a trip to see this marvel was the ideal honeymoon. From that time on, honeymooners have provided many of the train passengers to this scenic spot.

As the West was opened, other scenic attractions lured travelers. Because passengers wanted to observe the scenery and note historic sites, observation platforms and then observation cars with domed glass roofs were installed. Daniel Webster had started something when he insisted on sitting in a rocking chair fastened to a flatcar so that he would miss nothing on the ride from the Hudson River to Lake Erie. Ever since that time, until the automobile took over, the trains were widely used by vacationers and sightseers. In the early, less hurried days of travel, trains would often stop to permit photographers, wild-flower collectors, and others to dismount and indulge in their hobbies. Or the stop enabled passengers to stroll to a vantage point the train could not reach for a far-flung view of the country.

An early observation car — 1886. *Harper's*

Less active vacationists, especially the wealthy, used the trains to reach the watering places that were once the favorite vacation places of the wealthy. In the winter these people went south to resorts that offered special attractions. There was Aiken, South Carolina, once the terminal of the Charleston and Hamburg line. When polo was introduced in 1882, this town became the center for those who followed the sport. There they would spend the winter months watching the nation's top polo players practice, or strolling along the magnolia- and oak-shaded streets, or driving along the grassy roads, many of them still unpaved for the comfort of the horses. In March the gardens reached their peak of beauty, and soon after this the pleasure-seekers would reembark on the lavish trains and leave. Aiken has held its place as the center of winter polo activity, though the luxurious trains have vanished.

There were several Florida cities to which the wealthy fled each winter, riding south in whole trains devoted to their comfort. After Henry Flagler built the elegant Ponce de Leon Hotel in St. Augustine, to be followed by other swank hotels in Florida, such as the Royal Palm in Miami and the Royal Poinciana at Palm Beach, it was to that state that trainloads of vacationers went each fall.

But as summer approached, those who could afford to pick the climate and weather they preferred boarded the trains for the New England resorts. Saratoga Springs in eastern New York, north of Schenectady, was patronized by Indians because of the mineral waters which they believed were healthful. The second railroad in New York was built from Schenectady to the springs in 1832, and every summer afterward, trains brought their loads of summer visitors. With its casino, opera house, and racetrack, it was once one of the gayest centers in the country. There was Newport, Rhode Island, to which flocked in summer first the Southern cotton kings,

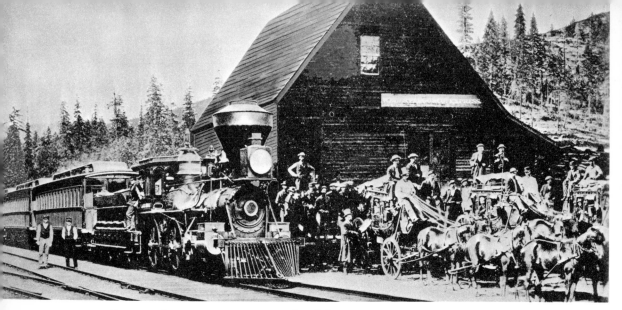

Stagecoaches meet a passenger train. Sightseers to the West's attractions rode the trains
as far as they could, then went the rest of
the way by stage. *Southern Pacific Company*

then the rich Bostonians, and finally, in its heyday, the Astors and
Vanderbilts and the other New Yorkers whose names are synony-
mous with wealth. There, on great estates, were built the palaces and
castles to which private cars brought their owners. The less affluent
came to their summer cottages in luxurious Pullmans.

The building of New York's second railroad to a resort points
up the part trains played in the development of recreation sites all
over the country. The Louisville and Nashville Railroad laid rails to
the Mammoth Cave in Kentucky long before this was made a national park. Henry Flagler understood the lure of unusual and mysterious regions when he tried to lay his line through the Everglades
of Florida. In the 1880's tourists would take the old Atlantic and
Pacific Railroad to Williams, Arizona, and then travel 60 miles by
stage to view the Grand Canyon. In the 1870's the North Pacific
Coast Railroad of California issued elaborate brochures advertising

the redwood forest and other scenic wonders along its route. The cover showed a tiny engine puffing its way among the giant trees, which thousands rode the train each year to see.

Where one of America's wonders could not be or had not been reached by rails, citizens from all parts of the country took a train to the nearest railroad station and then somehow — by horseback or muleback or stage — made their way to their destination. Americans were eager to see and know their country. Before the golden age of steam was over, the slogan See America First was coined by the Salt Lake City Chamber of Commerce and won a national award. The slogan was an outgrowth of what had actually been going on for fifty years, and so far the railroads had been the chief promoters and instruments of this activity.

During the golden age of steam many songs, plays, and stories were written about the railroads. This cover from the song "Number Twenty Nine" shows the type of illustration used on such ballads. *Library of Congress*

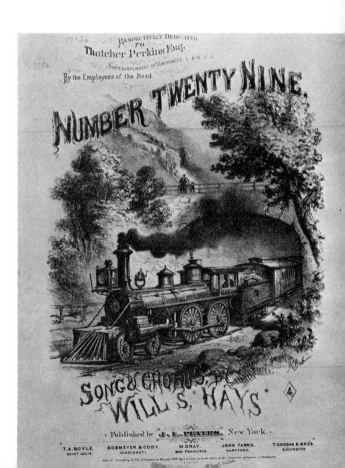

14

DISASTER RIDES THE RAILS

The golden age of steam ushered in also the dark age of railway disasters. Perhaps this was inevitable, all things considered.

During the first few years of railroad development there were few very bad accidents, in spite of the lack of safety features. Locomotives moved slowly, at 10 to 20 miles an hour. There was little travel at night, and comparatively few people were traveling. But as the weight of locomotives increased and their speed was stepped up to 30, 40, 70 miles an hour, with long trains of heavily loaded cars, almost any accident was bound to be disastrous.

Most accidents in the early years were caused by one of four incidents: derailing of a car, impaling of a car on a loose rail, hitting a cow or other animal, or colliding with another train. Such accidents were annoying but not often very serious. The public was duped into thinking that trains were safe.

In the 1850's things began to change. There was much more

travel at greater speeds over more miles of track. Much of the latter was single track, and there was no way for one train to pass another except on turnouts. These were short strips of extra track laid alongside the main track but connected to it by switches. Halfway between two turnouts a center post was set up. When two trains met on a single track, the one nearest the center post had to back up onto the siding to let the other pass. Since there was no system of communication between trains, such head-to-head meetings frequently occurred, and it was not always possible to stop before a collision. Even when the two engineers managed to halt their trains without harm, there was often a dispute as to which one should back up.

The first fatal accident on an American railroad was the explosion on the Best Friend of Charleston in June, 1831. The workman who caused it later died of his injuries. Because of the accident, the Charleston and Hamburg line, to which so many firsts are credited, issued the first set of rules governing railroad traffic. They ordered that no more than five passengers be allowed on any car. Locomotives were not to travel faster than 15 miles an hour if there was only one car with passengers, 12 miles an hour if there were two cars with passengers, and 10 miles an hour if three cars made up the train.

It was more than twenty years later before the public was shocked into a realization of how dangerous railroad travel could be. In 1853 a terrible accident occurred on the New York and New Haven at Norwalk, Connecticut. An engineer failed to see the warning signal and ran onto an open drawbridge. His train crashed, killing 40 and injuring twice that many. On August 29, 1855, the Camden and Amboy jumped the rails near Burlington, New Jersey, killing 21 and injuring 75. A broadside depicting the accident in a dramatic woodcut did much to arouse the public's indignation.

In May, 1858, two trains of the New York Central tried to pass each other on a wooden bridge near Utica. They did not collide, but the bridge broke under the weight of the two trains. Only a few weeks later a faulty rail caused another terrible accident. *Harper's Weekly* had long been pounding at the need for better safety precautions and more careful inspections. These two accidents, so close together, were the subject of a withering editorial. It blamed the railroads for not employing better materials, more safeguards, and more inspectors, even at a loss of revenue. Among other things, the editorial declared:

> It is not enough that the cars should be the most noisy, dusty and wearisome of carriages . . . . that the companies should absorb so much of the savings of honest laborers all over the land, and never return a dollar in dividends . . . all this is not enough, but every man who leaves a city by a

A defective rail upsets an engine on the Utah Central Railroad, about 1900. *Deseret News*

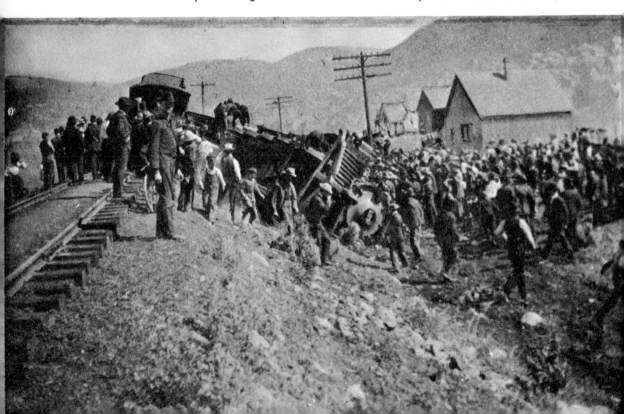

train must cast a lingering look behind, in sober sadness, doubting whether the chances of a safe arrival are not entirely against him.

Wrecks and accidents on the Long Island Railroad were so frequent they aroused little excitement until Thanksgiving Eve, 1865. Thanksgiving Day had not been widely or uniformly observed in this country. Some communities held no holiday; others had their autumn festival at any time they pleased. Until 1863 only one President had proclaimed a national day of thanksgiving. That was George Washington, in 1789. As editor of *Godey's Lady's Book*, Sarah Hale had for many years been agitating for a nationwide Thanksgiving Day in November. This campaign, like her constant urging of improvements in the railroads, was successful. She prevailed on President Lincoln to proclaim the fourth Thursday in November a national holiday on which all the people of the United States should refrain from work and join their families for a day of thanksgiving.

The idea was received with enthusiasm, and as in the previous two years, workers, released from work, crowded the trains out of the cities as they made their ways homeward. On this Thanksgiving Eve of 1865 the Manhattan-Hempstead local train was filled with tired but happy people. By this time block signals had been installed on the line, but now they failed to operate, and a fast express train rammed into the rear of the slower local. The toll from this accident was 77 killed, more than 100 injured.

By 1870 the American people had grown somewhat used to wrecks that resulted in many deaths and injuries. They were not, however, prepared for the disasters that were to scandalize the nation. All the comfort and luxury, the speed and convenience of the trains, could not obscure the dreadful toll they were taking.

Time and again the flimsy wooden bridges collapsed under the

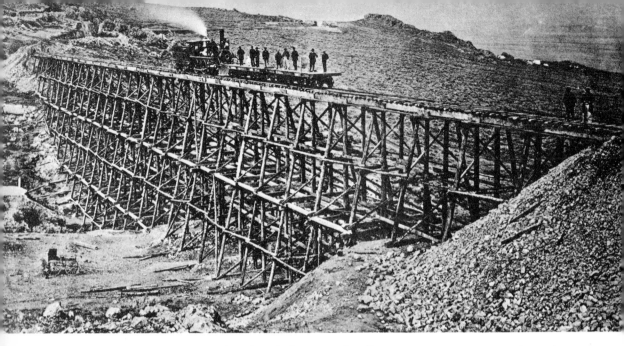

Wooden trestles like this, though they served well at one time, were constantly menaced by flying sparks or heavy windstorms.

weight of speeding trains. Such an accident occurred during a fearful storm on a cold December night in 1876. The great truss bridge at Ashtabula, Ohio, gave way under two locomotives and ten baggage and express cars of the Central Pacific Express. The cars were thrown into the river far below. There they burst into flames, cremating 92 persons.

The most famous bridge disaster was the Chatsworth wreck, which inspired a popular ballad that made the story known to people all across the country. The Toledo, Peoria and Western Railroad in 1887 started cheap summer excursions to Niagara Falls. On August 10 a doubleheader (with two engines) started out. Behind the locomotives were fifteen cars, packed full of excited vacationers. As it rushed through the hot summer night, the lead engine hit a wooden span over a shallow culvert. It got across safely, but the bridge had been weakened by charred planks caused by sparks from grass fires.

184

Under the impact of the second engine, it collapsed, piling the engine and cars into one flaming heap, in which 81 passengers were burned to death and many others fearfully injured.

Now newspaper editorials and magazine articles were not enough. Everywhere people wept as they heard the mournful ballad:

> From Peoria Town and hamlet
>   There came a happy throng
> To view the great Niagara Falls;
>   In joy they sped along.
>
> But Oh! how much of sorrow,
>   And Oh! how much of pain
> Awaited those who traveled on
>   That ill-fated railroad train!

In the final stanza the ballad maker's poetic license increased the number of casualties, though the actual toll was certainly awful enough:

> Over the land and water
>   The thrilling message crossed:
> The bridge was burned at Chatsworth
> And a hundred lives were lost!

The agitation for the abolishment of wooden bridges grew into a roar that could not be denied. Gradually stone and steel structures replaced the fragile wooden spans.

Increasing speed added its quota of accidents. One of the luxurious trains of the period was the Pacific Express of the New York Central and Hudson River Railroad. This crack train made the run from New York to Chicago in thirty-six hours, which made it a favorite of the public newly aroused to the excitement of speed. In February, 1871, it ran full speed and head on into a train of tank cars filled with petroleum. The oil was set on fire, and the Express was hurled, flaming, onto a frozen creek. The four cars at the rear were pushed to safety, but 22 passengers were burned to death in the other cars.

The wreck on the Chesapeake and Ohio near Hinton, West Virginia, was caused by a landslide. The train was running late, and to make up time, engineer George Alley was speeding along so fast he could not stop. He jumped from the cab but was so severely hurt he died a few hours later.

This wreck, too, was the subject of a ballad, one stanza of which says:

> Dear George leaped into the cab; the throttle he did pull;
> Old number Four started off like a mad and angry bull.
> Making up time, along she dashed, and into the rock she
> crashed;
> George Alley's head lay in the firebox, while the angry
> flames o'er flowed;
> "I'm glad I was born an engineer to die on the C and O
> road."

Another famous ballad about a speeding train told of the wreck of the Old 97. This occurred on September 27, 1903, when engineer Steve Broady was ordered to make up time between Spencer and Monroe, Virginia. Determined to cut an hour from the 166-mile run, Broady set out from Monroe at top speed, kept his fireman throwing coal into the firebox, and went rushing up and down hills and around

186

curves as fast as he could make the wheels turn. The result was disaster:

> He was flying downgrade at ninety miles an hour,
>   When his whistle began to scream, Whoo! Whooo!
> Steve was found in the wreck with his hand on the throttle
>   All scalded to death by the steam.

In spite of ballads and newspaper editorials, the accidents continued. In 1918 two terrible train disasters shook the nation. On June 22, just outside Ivanhoe, Indiana, a long train carrying the entire Hagenback-Wallace circus was stopped so the engineer could cool some overheated parts. There were fourteen flatcars loaded with equipment, seven cars filled with animals, and four Pullman cars in which the performers were peacefully sleeping. The train was made up of old, mostly wooden, cars, rebuilt for the circus.

The cars stood on the track in the darkness while the conductor worked on the hotbox. To avoid any possible danger, he sent the flagman back to set caution signals glowing behind the train. As the flagman finished the job, he looked up to see the glaring headlight of an oncoming train rushing at him through the night. He waved his red lantern frantically, yelling, though he knew his shouts could not be heard. The train did not slow down. As it hurtled past, the flagman flung a flaming fusee into the cab. It had no effect; the black monster rushed on, into the caboose of the stalled train. The circus cars were crumpled together and burst into flames. The screams of trapped people and animals filled the air.

Dozens of people were killed instantly; others and many of the animals were burned to death. Still others were critically injured. Altogether, 68 people died, and 127 were seriously injured. The animals suffered and died with the performers. It was the greatest circus disaster up to that time.

Less than three weeks later the worst railroad accident in the history of American railroads occurred at Nashville, Tennessee. Two fast trains collided head on, killing 101 and injuring 171. This disaster was due to faulty orders given the two engineers. Two other accidents during this golden age vie for the tragic honor of second place in the list of worst accidents. On August 7, 1904, at Eden, Colorado, a train was caught in a flood and washed downstream for three miles; 96 passengers were drowned. On March 1, 1910, at Wellington, Washington, another 96 lives were lost in the state's worst train wreck.

Altogether, during those fifty years, forty-one major railroad accidents killed nearly 2,000 people. No wonder the public demanded safety measures. In 1893 Congress did something about this problem. It passed the Railroad Safety Appliance Act, which was signed by President Benjamin Harrison on March 2 of that year. This act required that air brakes and automatic couplers be installed on all trains, both freight and passenger. The result was an almost immediate reduction in train accidents.

Since many of the worst accidents were caused by two trains colliding, it was necessary to devise some system that would keep this from happening. Various attempts had been made to keep trains apart by means of some sort of warning signal. Such a signal should impose a block between trains — this block would be one of space — a quarter of a mile, a half mile, or even many miles, according to the terrain and the density of traffic. Such a warning signal was called a block signal.

The primitive highball signal was one of the first devices used.

15

HEROES AND HEROINES

If there were accidents, there were also heroes and heroines who tried to prevent them. A favorite theme for stories, poems, and lithographs was the daring engineer or the brave heroine or the courageous youth or dog who risked life and limb in the cause of safety. And naturally, there were poems and posters showing the opposite side of the coin — the child killed by an onrushing train; the unhappy person throwing himself in front of a steaming locomotive.

The brave engineer was pictured climbing out on the cowcatcher to pick up a curly-headed little girl who had been caught on the slanting bars. Or he ran his engine through flood or fire to take help to a stricken village. Or he stuck to his post and died with his wrecked locomotive.

"Casey" Jones was the ideal hero engineer. He was a real person, whose name was John Luther Jones. He has been described as being more than six feet tall, with black hair and shrewd gray eyes. His

The only known full-face photograph of John Luther Jones, famous in song as the engineer who "mounted to the cabin . . . his orders in his hand." This photo was taken about 1897, while Casey was pulling freight on the Illinois Central at Jackson, Tennessee. *Illinois Central Railroad*

biography was written by Fred J. Lee, who worked on the Illinois Central when Casey was the crack engineer of that line. Lee says that Casey was born in Missouri in 1864. Later his family moved to Cayce, Kentucky, the town that gave the hero his nickname.

In 1888 Casey went to work as a fireman on the Illinois Central. Two years later, when only twenty-five years old, he was promoted to the responsible job of locomotive engineer. After some twelve years in this position, he was given the exciting task of piloting the company's fastest Chicago to New Orleans passenger train, the Cannonball. By this time he was one of the most experienced and responsible engineers in the country.

On April 29, 1900, Casey brought the northbound Cannonball into Memphis on time. There he learned that the engineer who was to take the southbound train out of Memphis was sick. Casey and his fireman, Sim Webb, were asked to take over the southbound run.

They accepted the job and, without getting any rest, set out, ninety-five minutes late, for New Orleans, 221 miles away.

Casey had orders to make up those ninety-five minutes. He told Webb to pile on the coal and opened the throttle. Away flew the Cannonball at 70 miles an hour. All went well till they reached the little town of Vaughan. Just before they came to the station, a torpedo on the track warned them to slow down. Four cars of a freight train too long for the siding were standing on the main track. Casey applied the brakes, and the Cannonball slowed to 50 miles an hour. It was not enough. Sim Webb, leaning out into the night, saw the danger and yelled for Casey to jump for his life. Casey shouted back, "You jump. I'll stay!" And stay he did, exerting all his strength on the air-brake control.

The Cannonball hit the freight cars with a mighy crash. Casey's engine was derailed and tipped over. A couple of freight cars and the

Engine 382 used on the Cannonball express, the New Orleans-bound passenger train which carried Casey Jones to the Promised Land in an accident at Vaughan, Mississippi. Not a passenger was injured. (Engineer is *not* Casey Jones in this photo.) *Illinois Central Railroad*

caboose were demolished. But no one was seriously injured save the brave engineer. His body was found in the wreckage. One hand still clutched the throttle; the other was clenched on the air-brake control. His action in staying with the engine had undoubtedly saved many lives. If he had jumped, the Cannonball would have gone on at its 50-mile speed, and the wreck would have been much more serious.

The story of Casey's heroism attracted a great deal of attention. A New Orleans newspaper called his act "a wonderful as well as a heroic piece of work." And a Negro trainman named Wallace Saunders put the event into a ballad that is considered the great rail-road classic. Parts of it will show how the story came to be known by thousands.

> Casey Jones, he mounted to the cabin;
> > Casey Jones, he had his orders in his hand.
> Casey Jones, he mounted to the cabin
> > And took his farewell journey to the Promised Land.

> He pulled up just before he reached the place,
> Old Number Four stared him right in the face;
> He turned to the fireman, "Boy, you'd better jump
> 'Cause there's two locomotives that are goin' to bump!"
> The fireman jumped, but Casey stayed —
> Tried to stop the Cannonball; he was not afraid.
> The two engines met; it's an old, old story
> Casey went to heaven in a blaze of glory.

George Alley, engineer on the ill-fated Chesapeake and Ohio, was another hero who, like Casey, stayed with his train while his fireman leaped to safety.

While the brave engineer was undoubtedly the hero of the rails, almost everyone who worked on the railroad seemed wonderful and romantic to the young people of the time. The conductor punching tickets, in his blue suit and brass buttons, appeared to have a remarkably easy and pleasant job. People had forgotten that up to the time of the Civil War most conductors and other railroad workers (like American policemen) refused to wear a distinctive uniform. In the young Republic, uniforms were detested as signs of class and servitude. A British visitor described the conductors on the early trains: "The American railway conductor is a non-descript being, half clerk, half guard, with a dash of the gentleman. . . . He is generally well dressed; sometimes wears a beard, and when off duty, he passes for a respectable personage at any of the hotels. . . ." But after he adopted the impressive blue uniform, he became a hero.

A famous conductor was Asa R. Porter, whose heroism was chiefly a quiet kind. During the Civil War he went out of his way to be helpful to the sick and wounded soldiers that rode his line. Porter was a conductor on the Steamboat Express, which from 1847 to 1937 made a daily afternoon run from Boston to Fall River, Massachusetts. There the passengers would take the ship *Queen of the Sound* for New York City. In the morning the boat train would take returning passengers from the ship to Boston. Porter was conductor on this boat train for thirty-two years and was a great favorite with the occasional, as well as the regular, customers.

There were other conductors who won a little fame for their quiet service, in times of trouble as well as peace. It was the conductor who soothed and pacified terrified passengers when danger made them panic. Thus, Conductor Barton herded 275 passengers into the baggage car and safety during a New England hurricane on September 21, 1938. The train was crossing the causeway over an arm of the ocean between Mystic, Connecticut, and Stonington, Rhode Island. The hurricane had swept all sorts of debris over the rails; even a house and a ship obstructed the way. Moreover, the waves were high, and the track was all underwater. Only in the baggage car was there safety, and with coolness and authority, Conductor Barton managed to crowd all the passengers through the swaying cars and the sea-washed vestibules into this refuge.

There are many stories of heroic citizens who saved a train from disaster. The first, probably, is about the act of Mrs. Silas Horton, whose home was near the railroad tracks near Owego, New York. One day early in 1854, Mrs. Horton saw that a huge tree had been blown down across the rails, just beyond a sharp curve that would prevent the engineer from seeing the obstruction in time to stop his train. And the train was coming! She could hear it chugging along, though it was still out of sight. The woman looked about for something with which to warn the engineer, but there seemed to be nothing except the clothes she had just hung on the line.

In her haste to get to the curve to give warning, she grabbed the nearest garment and ran. She reached the apex of the curve before the train and stood panting and waving her signal. The engineer saw it and stopped the train. He and the passengers gathered around the heroine to thank her. Everyone was too polite to mention the garment which had saved them from a wreck, and modest Mrs. Horton, when she became aware of it, crumpled it into the smallest possible ball and hid it under her apron. For the flag that saved the day was Mrs. Horton's red flannel petticoat.

The officials of the Erie Railroad recognized Mrs. Horton's deed. They sent her a letter of congratulation, a lifelong pass on the railroad, and a new dress.

Even more heroic was fifteen-year-old Kate Shelley of Iowa.

Kate lived on a small farm near the Chicago and Northwestern tracks over Haney Creek in the Des Moines Valley. Half a mile farther on, the tracks were carried over the Des Moines River on a wooden bridge.

On the night of July 6, 1881, a fearful storm hit the valley. Uprooted trees were swept along on the swollen creeks and rivers. The flimsy bridges and trestles were in danger. Kate sat in the cottage, listening to the storm. She heard a pilot locomotive go past the house and onto the trestle over Honey Creek. She was a railroad man's daughter and knew that this little locomotive with its crew of four had been sent out to test the safety of the bridge over the river before the fast Atlantic Express, with its load of passengers, was to arrive.

As Kate listened, the sounds of the storm were suddenly pierced by a loud crash, the hissing of steam, and the ringing of the engine's bell. She knew what had happened. The pilot had crashed through the flimsy trestle; the crew must be in the raging creek.

Kate knew what she had to do. She had to get across the river to the Moingona station beyond to get help for the men and to stop the Express before it thundered onto the broken span. This would not have been an easy task, even in calm daylight. To keep pedestrians from using the railroad bridge, much of the planking had been removed, leaving only the ties with the spaces between open to the river below. Kate, like others, had walked the ties in the daytime; now she must do so by night and in a howling wind and pelting rain. But she did not hesitate. She took a lantern from its hook, lighted it, and set out.

As she passed Honey Creek, a flash of lightning showed her the broken trestle and two of the pilot engine's crew clinging to trees on the creek bank, just above the swirling water. She knew she had to hurry. Those men could not hold on for long.

197

Kate reached the river bridge and started across, picking her way carefully by the feeble light of her lantern. She had gone only halfway across when the wind blew out the flickering light, and she was left in darkness, save for the occasional flashes of lightning. She could no longer trust her feet to find the next tie, and a slip would be fatal. She got to her knees and slowly, painfully, crept along the rails. Crawling there above the river in the darkness was a terrifying experience.

Kate finally reached the far end of the bridge, got to her feet, and ran along the muddy road to the little station. There she panted out her story. The stationmaster sent a crew back to rescue the two men; two had been swept away and were lost. Then he made ready to flag down the Express, which was now due at any minute.

Kate Shelley was a true heroine and has been honored by railroad men for her courageous act. The Brotherhood of Railway Trainmen

An artist's sketch of Kate Shelley creeping across the railroad bridge over the Des Moines River during a fearful night storm. *Order of Railway Conductors and Brakemen*

Kate Shelley, whose heroic action prevented a terrible railroad disaster. *Order of Railway Conductors and Brakemen*

named a lodge for her. Newspapers and private individuals wrote letters, stories, articles, and poems about her. The Chicago *Tribune* sponsored a fund to help Kate's family. The State of Iowa gave her a gold medal and $200. The schoolchildren of Dubuque gave her a medal, and a Kate Shelley fountain was placed in the city park. The employees of the railroad company gave her a gold watch, and the officials presented a lifelong pass over their lines.

The fifteen-year-old farm girl had actually performed the heroic deed many young people dreamed of doing. Unlike "Casey Jones," the poems telling about it are scarcely known today, and so her act has almost been forgotten. But at one time children recited verses and read stories about Kate on school programs across the country. One poem by Eugene J. Hall was especially popular. Another, less well known, ends:

199

Let others sing of heroes;
   Such praise is due, I guess.
But I extol Kate Shelley
   Who saved the Fast Express!

A hobo called Springfield Mike also saved a fast express train in May, 1908. He was strolling along the tracks of the New Haven line near Torrington, Connecticut, when he came across a broken rail. At that moment he heard the whistle of the train. He pulled off his red bandana, stood on the tracks, and waved it while he yelled for the engineer to stop. The train stopped, and Mike was surrounded by grateful crew and passengers. They offered the hero gifts of money, but he would take nothing. He felt that he had now paid the railroad for some of the free rides he had taken in empty baggage cars or on the rods.

A hero of a different sort was John Henry, the "steel-driving man," whose story in song is almost as well known as "Casey Jones." The steel driver is the man who uses a heavy sledgehammer to drive a steel drill into solid rock to make a hole in which dynamite can be placed. In mountainous regions he goes ahead of the grader and tracklayer.

The story of John Henry comes from the West Virginia hills, where the Big Bend Tunnel on the Chesapeake and Ohio, near Hillsdale, was blasted through granite mountains. While this tunnel was being constructed, the steel drill was introduced to cut down the hard work of the hand-driven drill. John Henry could not accept the fact that a machine could outdo a man. He challenged the steam drill to a contest of strength and speed. The drill accepted the dare, and they set to work.

John Henry said to his captain,
    "A man ain't nothing but a man.
And before I'll let any old steam drill beat me
    I'll die with my hammer in my hand."

The steam drill was set on the right side;
    John Henry, he sat on the left.
He said, "I'll beat that old steam drill down
    Or hammer my fool self to death!"

John Henry took two twenty-pound hammers,
    A twenty-pound hammer in each hand;
He beat that steam hammer twelve inches to nine,
    And he died with those hammers in his hand.

They took John Henry to the graveyard;
    And they buried him deep in the sand,
And every locomotive that goes roaring by — Whooo! Whoo!
    Whistles, "There lies a steal driving man!"

People were not the only heroes of the great days of steam. Sometimes the railroad company itself proved to be heroic. This was the case in eastern Nevada, when the Southern Pacific was realigning tracks in 1904, but the story has not often been told.

Soon after the discovery of gold in California, a party of emigrants was following the usual trail along the Humboldt River. It was ambushed by Paiute Indians near a shallow crossing, known as the Gravelly Ford. In the fight young Lucinda Duncan was killed. She was buried, and the company moved on.

In 1904 the Southern Pacific was realigning the old Central Pacific tracks across Nevada. Workmen came upon the grave, above which a weather-beaten headboard was still standing crookedly. The inscription gave only the girl's name. The grave had to be moved, so the workmen carefully took up the remains and reburied them. The railroad company erected a cross above the little mound and undertook to keep the grave in perpetual repair. For many years, passengers were given a small pamphlet telling the story, while conductors pointed out the cross. Some unknown writer put the story into verse:

THE MAIDEN'S GRAVE

What is that crucifix gleaming so whitely,
　　Here in the desert standing so brave?
Let us go softly, let us go lightly,
　　To read its inscription, "The Maiden's Grave."

The cross marking the Maiden's Grave in northern Nevada.

Who was the Maiden? Why is she lying
　　Here on the desert so lonely and still,
While around the cross the eagles are flying
　　And the coyote howls mournfully from yonder hill?

Ask whom you will, they'll tell you only
　　The story's forgotten; no facts were saved;
Only the cross knows, standing so lonely,
　　Guarding so tenderly the Maiden's Grave.

Dogs, too, became heroes. A popular subject for posters, lithographs, and even embroidered sofa pillows was a big, shaggy dog, perhaps a Newfoundland, pulling a careless child from in front of an engine.

So, in addition to its chief service of transportation, the railroads gave another value to American life. Its heroes and heroines, whether actual or fictional, offered romance and inspiration to young people, who were kept constantly aware of the brave deeds that occasionally occurred along the right-of-ways.

That there was another side to the story, most older people well knew, and *their* magazines and newspapers carried woodcuts, cartoons, and biting editorials on the subject. But even the authors of the bitterest attacks on the evil practices of railroad companies — the failure to adopt safety devices, overcapitalization, bilking of emigrants, land grabbing, overcharging, and so on — even these people would be damp-eyed as they watched the play *The Limited Mail*, with little Nellie saving the fast express. Or they would beam proudly as their small son, all slicked up for the occasion, recited "The Engineer's Story," or a beribboned little girl sang sadly "In the Baggage Coach Ahead."

16

BANDITS PLAGUE THE TRAINS

The golden age of steam spawned a less pleasant phenomenon — the train robber gang. As travel increased and richer cargoes and more valuable mail were carried over the rails, the trains became the targets for outlaws, particularly in the Middle West and the Far West.

Travelers had always been the prey of the lawless. In Europe there had been highwaymen and footpads, who made a business of robbing the stagecoaches and the wayfarers. New England had its highwaymen, with Captain Lightfoot probably the best known. In the West the coaches carrying gold or silver from the mines to mill or railroad had long been harassed by bandits. But for about forty years after the introduction of steam trains, the Iron Horse had looked too formidable to be attacked. This happy state was not to last.

The first holdup of an American train took place on October 6, 1866, near Seymour, Indiana. The evening run on the Ohio and Mississippi Railroad, with an express car and a baggage car, pulled out of Seymour and rolled eastward. From the coach just behind the express car came two masked men. Up to this time the doors of express cars had never been locked, so the two bandits had no trouble entering. At gunpoint they took the keys from the messenger, opened the safe, and removed about $1,300. Then they pulled the bell cord to signal the engineer to stop. As the train ground to a halt, the robbers heaved out an unopened safe and leaped to the ground.

No one on the train had any idea what to do. They went on to the next station and sent back a posse on a handcar. When these men searched the site of the holdup, the bandits had disappeared in the darkness. The unopened safe had been left behind.

A family named Reno lived near Seymour. There were five brothers and one sister. Four of the brothers, Frank, John, Simeon, and William, were always in trouble. But Clinton refused to have anything to do with his brothers' shenanigans. They scornfully called

Frank Reno, whose gang staged the first American train robbery. *Pinkerton's National Detective Agency*

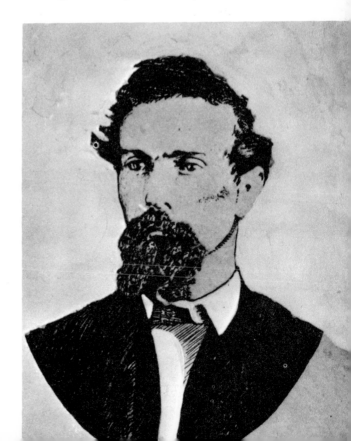

him the honest Reno. The train robbery was immediately laid at the Renos' door. The four bad Renos and their pal Frank Sparks were arrested. But they were released on bail, and their trial was never held.

For two years the four Renos and their pals terrorized Indiana and made forays into Iowa and Missouri. Train holdups were interspersed with bank robberies and murders. The Pinkerton Detective Agency was called in by the railroad company, but the depredations went on. At last the people of the area formed the Southern Indiana Vigilance committee. Members wore their coats wrong side out and covered their faces with red flannel masks so they could not be identified.

The vigilantes' first catch was a trio of train robbers who had just been arrested. They were taken from the law officers and lynched from a tree near the crossroads, giving that place the name of Hangman's Crossing, by which it is still known. A few days later three more men were caught and hanged, but so far no Renos. They were all safe in the Jefferson jail, awaiting trial. On the night of December 11, 1868, the vigilantes broke into the jail and there lynched Frank, William, and Simeon Reno and Charlie Anderson. The Reno gang was ended.

This earliest train robbing gang, like many to follow, was made the subject of a ballad. It was once popular in southern Indiana. Each stanza ended:

> For the Scarlet Masks are riding
> To wipe out the Reno Gang.

For a year or two, trains were not bothered by robbers, and then the real trouble began. There were train holdups in Kentucky and

Tennessee and out West in Nevada. The plague spread to New England, but the Middle West bore the brunt of this outlawry.

It was through the Middle West that Jesse James and his brother Frank, the Youngers — Cole, Bob, John, and Jim — Sam Bass and his gang operated. Utah, Wyoming, Colorado, and Idaho were the stamping ground of Butch Cassidy and the Wild Bunch. In California the Sontag brothers ran amok for a brief period. All these characters took up train robbery as a way of life. If wrecks and murders were included, that did not bother them at all.

The James-Younger gang had been robbing banks for some time when, on July 21, 1873, they held up their first train. They chose the Chicago, Rock Island and Pacific. As the cars sped peacefully along near Adair, Iowa, the outlaws waited in the thick trackside underbrush just beyond a curve, which would prevent the engineer from observing anything amiss. Across the track a stout rope was stretched, almost invisible in the twilight. The train rounded the curve, hit the rope, and was overturned, killing the engineer.

A Union Pacific express car after the holdup at Wilcox, Wyoming, on June 2, 1899. Dynamiting the car was a favorite method of getting at the safe. *Union Pacific Railroad Museum Collection*

A number of men came out of the brush, rifled the baggage and express cars, and then went through the passenger coaches, relieving the travelers of purses, wallets, jewelry, and watches. How much was obtained is not known, but it is estimated at around $4,000.

The Pinkertons were called in by the company, and in the resulting struggles three of the detectives and one of the gang — Frank Younger — were killed. But the holdups continued for three years. On September 7, 1876, ten members of the gang tried to hold up the bank at Northfield, Minnesota. They did not even get into the vault. Angry citizens took up their guns, shot down three of the bandits, and injured three Youngers, who were later caught and jailed. Bob died in prison, and Jim later committed suicide. Cole served his sentence until 1901, when he was pardoned. He became a showman and lecturer, all his wickedness seemingly forgotten.

Frank and Jesse James escaped the Northfield attack and went on to commit three more train robberies before Jesse was shot and killed by his cousin, Bob Ford, on April 3, 1882. Frank turned respectable and lived until 1915.

A number of ballads were composed about the Jameses and the Youngers. Jesse came in for the greatest share; for some reason he had captured the imagination of many people who excused his robbing and murdering with silly, sentimental claims that he was good-hearted or that he robbed the rich to give to the poor. Neither was true. The whole gang were simply mean, wicked killers. Some never forgave Bob Ford for killing Jesse in order to get the reward. The most famous Jesse James ballad has the refrain:

The dirty little coward
That murdered Mr. Howard
And laid Jesse James in his grave.

Cole Younger, the one who turned respectable, is described in a ditty:

I am a bandit highwayman, Cole Younger is my name,
For many a depredation I brought my friends to shame.

And after several stanzas:

The Union Pacific Railroad, their passengers we surprised —
The fear of our bloody hands brought the tears into their eyes.
The engineer and fireman were killed; the conductor escaped
    with his life.
And now their bodies are lying beneath Nebraska's burning
    skies.

A year after the James-Younger gang was blasted at Northfield, a sixteen-year-old country boy set out to follow their example. On September 18, 1877, Sam Bass and his pal Joe Collins, with four other men, held up the Union Pacific express when it stopped to take on water at Big Springs, Nebraska. The robbers found $60,000 stashed away in little boxes on the floor of the express car. Because this car always carried valuables, it was the first goal of any holdup. After taking the money, the bandits went through the coaches robbing the passengers. This was Sam's first train robbery, though he had had some experience in holding up stagecoaches. He thought this new business was easier than the old and decided to become a train robber for the rest of his life.

It wasn't to be a long one. Sam died from a Texas ranger's bullet on his twenty-seventh birthday. His success as a train robber had been nothing to brag about. After that first rich haul, he never again found much treasure on the trains he held up. His ballad tells us:

Sam Bass was born in Indiana; that was his native home,
And at the tender age of sixteen, young Bass began to roam.
He first came out to Texas, a cowboy for to be —
A fellow with a kinder heart you'd seldom hope to see.

These were the most noted train robbers of the Middle West, though there were others. There were the Farrington brothers — Levi and Hilary — Tom Nixon, Al Jennings, and various loners or minor members of outlaw bands. But these were never great threats to the trains, and they died poor and obscure, their days of banditry short and unprofitable.

Butch Cassidy and the Wild Bunch were never as widely known as some of the Middle West gangs, but in Utah and Wyoming they were once the most publicized group of outlaws. They never did attain the renown of having a popular ballad sung about them, and only in the West were the stories of their Robin Hood character circulated.

Butch's real name was George LeRoy Parker — a gentle name for an outlaw! He was born on April 6, 1866, on his father's lonely ranch in southern Utah. There the boy grew up to become a cattle rustler and gunfighter. Robbing trains was a sideline with Butch, and never very profitable.

Butch Cassidy's Wild Bunch: standing, Bill Carver, Harvey Logan; sitting, Harry Long-baugh, Ben Kilpatrick and George LeRoy Parker (Butch Cassidy). *Union Pacific Rail-road*

When he decided on a career of outlawry, he adopted the last name of his instructor in wickedness, Mike Cassidy. Then he set about collecting a group of tough characters, including Harry Long-baugh, Harvey Logan, and Harry Tracy. On November 3, 1887, Butch and a companion held up the Denver and Rio Grande train, five miles out of Grand Junction, Colorado, not far from the Utah border. The express messenger refused to open the safe, and the bandits decided to let him live and to forget about the loot. Their first train robbery netted nothing but experience. The incident has often been told in Utah to prove what a good heart Butch had.

Butch was never as successful as a train robber as he was as a cattle rustler or bank bandit. Still, he organized the Train Robbers' Syndicate and made a few large hauls. Altogether, though, he never reached his dream of being known as the great train bandit. His lack of success was due largely to the untiring work of such Pinkerton men as Charlie Siringo, the cowboy detective, and W. O. Sayles. Butch's end has been a matter of much dispute, though now it is generally accepted that he was killed by law officers in South America in 1903. In 1968 a motion-picture company finally made a film based on Butch's life. On location in southern Utah, the company honored Butch's youngest sister, born in 1884, who stoutly maintained in interviews that "Butch was a mighty fine boy."

California's best-known train robbers were the Sontag brothers, George and John. They began their notorious career in Minnesota and Wisconsin in the early 1890's. After moving to California, they began operations by holding up a train at the Collis station in Fresno county. They blasted the express car with dynamite and took some $5,000 from the Wells, Fargo safe.

It was decided that the job must have been done by the Sontags, and a posse set out after them. They were already on the wanted list because of their doings in their old home area. The bandits fled into the hills, and there they were joined by a farmer named Chris Evans, who brought along his gun to help the robbers.

For two or three days the chase went on; then the trio was trapped in a barn. George Sontag was captured and put in prison. His brother and Evans shot their way out, killing a deputy sheriff. For nine months these two eluded capture by posses made up of local law officers, newly sworn deputies, Pinkerton men, Wells, Fargo men, and a few Indian trackers. Up and down the San Joaquin Valley went the chase. Several times the outlaws were almost caught, but they always managed to shoot their way clear, wounding, in all, seven men.

The showdown came in June in a pitched battle on Sampson's Flat. Two deputies were killed, and so was John Sontag. Chris Evans was captured and sentenced to life imprisonment. When George heard of his brother's death, he tried to escape from Folsom Prison and was shot down.

The Sontags became widely known because the famous newspaper columnist Ambrose Bierce published a great deal about them. He even used a letter in rhyme, written by Chris Evans' daughter Eva, who was John Sontag's sweetheart. A Fresno paper also carried a poetic tribute to John Sontag, which began:

> In his narrow grave, the bandit
> Lies in calm, untroubled rest;
> Dreary spread the plains about him
> Toward the mountains of the West.

And ended:

> Came that last and desperate battle
> In the darkness of the night
> Flames from rifles lit the ledges.
> In the dawn of morning light
> All was silent. It was over;
> Far away, beneath the shade
> Of the rugged desert cedar
> Is the bandit Sontag's grave.

One more train robber must be mentioned because of the exciting train chase that ended his career.

Oliver Curtis Perry was born in Wyoming, but he made his reputation in New York State. On September 29, 1891, he sawed a hole in the express car of the New York Central's fast express from New York City to Albany. He crawled through this hole and ordered the surprised messenger to hand over the cash and jewels in the safe. This was his first robbery, and because of Perry's unique method of gaining access to the express car, it received much publicity.

A few months later he robbed the same train again. Then on September 20, 1892, he held up the New York Express Company's car at Lyons, New York. It was this holdup that really brought him to the nation's attention.

Perry pistol-whipped the messenger into unconsciousness, but before he passed out, the beaten man managed to pull the bell cord to signal the conductor. The conductor came, peered through the

ROB'T A. PINKERTON, Gen'l Supt.   WM. A. PINKERTON, Gen'l Supt.

EASTERN DIVISION, NEW YORK.   WESTERN DIVISION, CHICAGO, ILL'S.

PINKERTON'S NATIONAL DETECTIVE AGENCY

"WE NEVER SLEEP."   FOUNDED BY ALLAN PINKERTON, 1850.

NEW YORK: BOSTON: PHILADELPHIA: CHICAGO: ST PAUL: KANSAS CITY: DENVER:
66 Exchange Place, 43 & 44 Court Street, 441 Chestnut Street, 191 & 193 Fifth Avenue. Germania Bank Bl'g. 105 & 107 W. Sixth Street, Opera House Block
Geo. D. Bangs, Supt.   John Cornish, Supt.   Frank Murray, Supt.   Jno. C. McGinn, Supt.   C. H. Efflsheimer, Supt.   Jas. McFarland, Supt.
PORTLAND, ORE., Marquam Block, Th.M. F. Cleary, Supt.

ATTORNEYS FOR THE AGENCY.

D. W. Munn. Chicago. Ills.   Clarence A. Seward. New York.   Geo. S. Graham. Philadelphia.

$1,000 REWARD !

ARREST

OLIVER CURTIS PERRY,

alias James Curtis Perry, alias " Curt " Perry,

alias Oliver Moore,

FOR TRAIN ROBBERY.

The above likeness is a good one but flatters. His face is not so full and the lips are thinner.

Oliver Curtis Perry is described as 26 years of age, 5 feet 6 to 7 inches in height, slight build, weighing about 130 lbs., dark brown hair, small moustache, inclined to be sandy, (probably now shaved off,) brown eyes; high, white forehead, with wrinkles between eyes, giving his face a troubled and thoughtful expression ; thin lips, rather long nose, slim white hands, with enlarged knuckles from hard work. Has a scar about three inches long on upper part of forehead, which is noticeable when his hat is off ; also has scar on left arm and above right nipple. He is gentlemanly, polite and effeminate in manner, but acts nervous and uneasy; has a girlish voice, dresses in dark clothes, invariably wears gloves, and is noticeably particular about keeping his hands clean. Had gold open face watch, 14 karat, stemwinder, size 18, Samuel C. Tappen, Troy, N. Y., maker, name on dial and movement, nickel movement, case No. 14,608, movement No. 2,672,281 ; also a gold watch chain. Also wears a ring with stone on little finger of right hand, (probably now wearing diamonds).

From information received Perry may use any of the following names :

Oliver, Curtis, Perry, Haswell, Van Allen, Havens, Hamlin, Allen, Gavens, James, James Curtis, James Perry, James Curtis Perry, Oliver Moore.

Perry is said to have been at one time a cattle herder (cowboy). He has also been convicted and sentenced twice for burglary, and while in prison learned the shoemaker's trade.

Recently he has been a freight and passenger brakeman.

He professes religion, and will try to impose on ministers and class leaders of churches, particularly Presbyterian.

Poster put out by Pinkerton's for the capture of Oliver Curtis Perry. *Pinkerton's National Detective Agency* door window, and saw what was happening. He signaled the engineer to stop the train, but when this was done and a search made, no trace of the bandit could be found.

A little farther on, they came into the station at Lyons, where a posse of fifty angry men, who had heard of the holdup, was waiting to board a special train on which it could return to hunt in the woods for the robber. The conductor, who had had a good look at Perry, spied him among the crowd at the station, acting as if he were one of the posse. The sly robber had simply taken a seat in a Pullman car and passed as a regular traveler during the search of the train. The conductor pointed at the bandit and shouted, "There he is!"

Perry leaped away from the crowd, jumped up into the cab of a waiting freight engine, opened the throttle, and went scooting down the track. The posse, yelling, climbed onto the special train which stood on tracks parallel to those used by the fleeing bandit. Their engineer set out after the freight engine. Down the tracks they raced, the posse men with guns aimed to fire when they came close enough. But Perry was also ready and answered shot for shot. The pursuing engine came up alongside the pursued, and some of the posse made ready to jump aboard the other cab.

Suddenly Perry jumped on the air-brake control, put his engine in reverse, and fled backward up the track. The amazed posse instantly followed the robber's example, and they, too, went racing in reverse along the rails. As soon as they neared their quarry, he changed directions again and shot past the yelling posse as he sped forward. Time and again, Perry managed to rocket past the angry, shouting pursuers, but the engineer on the posse's train was almost as quick and kept close. After a while, with all his bullets used up, Perry saw that this crazy back-and-forth race could not save him. Near Newark he abandoned the engine and fled into the woods.

At a farmhouse Perry stole a horse and buggy and went racing down a narrow woodland road. The entire posse had given chase. The men commandeered another horse and buggy and followed Perry. Finally, the robber was cornered in a swamp. He threw his empty gun away and surrendered. He was taken back to New York, tried, convicted, and sentenced to forty-nine years in prison. He tried to commit suicide. He succeeded in putting out both eyes and lived in solitary confinement, blind and lonely, until his death in 1930 at the age of sixty-four.

Perry's one amusement in prison was the writing of poetry — of sorts. Much of this was sent to nearby newspapers, and some was published.

Like other regions of the country, the South, too, had its most publicized train robber. This was a Negro outlaw named Morris Slater, known throughout the South as Railroad Bill. He was a powerfully built fellow, thirty-eight to forty years of age, and he always carried a .38 Winchester rifle and two revolvers. For three years, from 1894 to 1897, he kept Alabama and Florida in a state of terror.

Railroad Bill was given his nickname because of his penchant for robbing freight and express cars. The freight cars were his specialty. He would climb into one as it rolled by and throw out the merchandise along the right-of-way. Later he would pick up the loot. Railroad officials and local law officers tried to catch the fellow, but their lack of success made people think the robber led a charmed life. Legends grew up about him. It was said that he could change his form into that of a bloodhound and run with the dogs set out on his trail. Or that he could turn into a horse or cow and calmly watch the posses race past.

During the pursuit of the robber, a deputy sheriff of Baldwin County, Alabama, was killed. The people were determined to avenge their officer. A capable Negro detective was employed to become friendly with the outlaw and then, when he was off guard, arrest him at gunpoint. But Railroad Bill was never off guard. And suddenly reports from the detective, Mark Stinson, stopped coming into headquarters. Stinson was never seen again, alive or dead.

Finally, Railroad Bill killed Sheriff McMillen, and the hunt became even more active. A large number of citizens were deputized to get Bill whenever and wherever they found him. A group of these deputies discovered their prey in a little store at Atmore, Alabama. He was sitting on an upended box, calmly eating crackers and cheese. The officers crept stealthily around the store. Constable J. S. McGowan raised his gun and shot. The storekeeper, discovering the deputies and knowing that help was at hand, had his gun ready and fired at the same time. Railroad Bill was hit by both bullets. He slumped to the floor, dead.

By 1900 the general public was tired of the train robbers. Better law enforcement agencies were employed, better means of communication helped, and the general attitude had changed from one of romantic acceptance to one of determined resistance. More and more robbers were caught and executed in one way or another. More care was taken of valuable cargoes, so the holdups became less profitable. The career of train robber grew less and less glamorous and rewarding.

In 1900 there were twenty-nine holdups; in 1905 there were five. There have been some since then, but nothing in America has equaled a holdup in England — the greatest train robbery of all time. On August 8, 1963, near Cheddington, a group of highwaymen robbed the crack mail train of more than $7,000,000. Some of this has been recovered, and a dozen men have been convicted and given long prison sentences.

17

RAILROADS TODAY

Stewart Holbrook, writing in 1947, scolded those unpleasant prophets who were then predicting that the railroads were doomed. He said, "The present writer believes that 1967 will find trains still rolling in great numbers across and up and down the continent."

He was right. Trains were still rolling in 1967 and in 1968, with no signs of immediate extinction. Still, some of the trains Holbrook knew really had disappeared. Such luxury trains as the Twentieth Century Limited of the New York Central Railroad could no longer be enjoyed by travelers who were glad to pay the extra $5 charge just to ride on this Waldorf-Astoria on wheels. When passengers entrained at the Grand Central Terminal in New York City, a red carpet was unrolled for them to walk on. No railroad company today can indulge in such extravagance. And other luxury trains have disappeared: the Baltimore and Ohio's Royal Blue, from which on August 15, 1947, the first commercial radiotelephone call from a train was made; the Southern Pacific's Golden State, which gave passengers from Chicago to Los Angeles the finest accommodations and service to be found on rails. These and others like them have been discontinued in the interest of economy.

Most major lines still maintain luxury trains, especially for long runs, but many of the extras have been eliminated. The Union Pacific's City of Los Angeles offers beautiful domeliners with dining rooms under a glass roof high above the passing landscape. The Santa Fe's San Francisco Chief makes the run from Chicago to San Francisco in forty-seven and a half hours; its Pullmans feature radio, recorded music, and courier nurse service. Its schedule is so arranged that passengers can enjoy all the scenic beauties of the trip.

These are examples of the best in today's train service. What happened between the twenties and the sixties? Well, there were two

A Milwaukee Road speedliner flashes along on a fast daytime schedule between Chicago, Milwaukee, St. Paul, and Minneapolis. These trains have reclining seats, dining cars with stainless-steel kitchens, a sky-top lounge, air conditioning, a public address system, and radio. *Chicago, Milwaukee, St. Paul and Pacific Railroad*

world wars. Though the first one took place just before the twenties (1914–18), its effects were felt for several years, and the depression that followed in the late twenties was a real setback to all kinds of travel and to all railroad improvement and expansion.

Then, from 1941 to 1945, the United States was involved in the Second World War. Again the railroads were preempted to serve the war effort. Growth and development had to be subordinated to the one great purpose of winning the war. But aside from these interruptions, research and experimentation were going on with the aim of making railroad travel safer, more convenient, and more comfortable.

The passenger cars of today are not very different from the better cars of the early part of the century, though there have been some refinements. The seats are now covered with synthetic materials that

Modern lavatories are clean and convenient. *Western Pacific Railway*

Railroad lounge cars have comfortable chairs, small tables for snacks, and recent magazines for the passengers to read. *Union Pacific Railroad.*

wear longer, look better, and resist soil more effectively than the old plush upholstery. They are padded with foam rubber, unknown only a few years ago, and adjust into comfortable couches for sleeping. Fluorescent lighting, air conditioning, and steam heat add to the comfort of passengers. A tank of ice water with sanitary paper cups is in every car. Lavatory facilities are modernized and have electric outlets for razors, paper towels, and separate basins for brushing teeth.

Pullman cars are more luxurious, with more roomettes than before. These roomettes give the passenger seclusion and comfort on overnight trips. Some have their own private lavatory. Lounge cars have upholstered seats, ashtrays, and small tables at which refreshments can be served. The dining car is supplemented by a snack car, in which the food is less expensive, the service less elaborate. Some trains also carry an automatic sandwich and drink dispenser, where food may be obtained at very reasonable prices.

A meal on a train is a real treat. Here young passengers wait to be served in an all-electric dining car. *Chesapeake and Ohio Railway*

Some trains carry automatic food dispensers for the convenience of day coach passengers. *Southern Pacific Company*

Most major lines have dome observation cars placed here and there throughout the train, so that those who wish to may view the scenery from comfortable seats.

There have been many complaints that attention to the passenger has sadly deteriorated during the past years, that cars are not kept clean, that seats are not repaired, that equipment has not been replaced or kept up to modern standards. This is undoubtedly true of some small lines which have found their former passengers now using the automobile or bus for short runs. But on most major lines this is not the case, and some have even tried to compete with the services offered by jet airliners. The Seaboard Coast Line runs a luxurious special to Florida resorts that would amaze even the rich private car owners of an earlier day. For on this train there are such attractions as full-length movies, sing-alongs, bingo games, and fashion shows.

From the dome cars of the California Zephyr, passengers get wide, clear views of the magnificent scene through which this train passes. *Western Pacific Railway*

However, the great changes in modern trains have not been in the passenger cars. The freight cars and, most of all, the locomotives have been modified.

With airlines, buses, and private cars competing for the patronage of the traveler, more and more of today's railroad revenues come from carrying freight. Because of this, a great deal of attention has been given to the subject of how best to handle and move cargoes of various kinds. During the past twenty years more than 1,000,000 new and improved freight cars have been placed on the rails. About two-thirds of the money spent each year by the railroads goes into this part of their service.

As far back as 1865 it was recognized that special cargoes needed special cars. In November of that year the first specially built tank car for oil was put into service at Titusville, Pennsylvania. Today

Trainloads of sugar beets are carried from the farms to the factories. *Northern Pacific Railway*

A steel span for a new bridge is loaded onto a gondola and flatcar. Transporting such gigantic objects is one job the railroads do today. *Reading Railroad*

huge, sleek tanks carry oil, whale-shaped tankers are used for various fluids, and a handsome, oval-shaped tanker is filled with dry stuffs that are shipped in bulk. Boxcars the size of a house carry automobile parts and canned goods. Hoppers that dwarf earlier cars of this type hold 100 tons or more of grain, flour, or sugar.

Two types of cars are really new: the multilevel car for moving automobiles and the piggyback carrier. The multilevel car is essentially a flatcar with a framework on which automobiles are placed in rows, one above the other. Each car can carry from 12 to 15 automobiles, whereas the earlier boxcar could move only 4. Out of Detroit now roll brightly colored trains, each carrying as many as 1,800 shining new automobiles — as much as 300 trucks could move along a highway. With some 5,000,000 new cars being manufactured every year, it was necessary to find a way to distribute them to dealers more safely, quickly, and efficiently than the old methods.

Large doors on these big boxcars make loading and unloading easy. Heavy springs give modern appliances a smooth, safe ride with a minimum of damage. *Union Pacific Railroad*

A modern ore car has a hopper bottom so the ore can be easily dumped. *Chicago and North Western Railway*

The three-level rack car is one of the innovations in freight handling. *Santa Fe Railway*

The piggyback traffic has developed chiefly since 1955. In this service, loaded truck trailers or filled containers the size of the old boxcar are loaded onto flatcars and transported to their destination. Since many such trailers and containers can be carried on one long train, it keeps hundreds of trucks off the highways. In the piggyback system, a truck brings a loaded trailer from some industry that is not located near a railroad. The loaded trailer is hoisted onto the flatcar that is to move it to a distant city or a seaport. Since it would take 200 trucks and trailers to move as much freight along the highways as a 100-car piggyback train can move over rails, this new service not only reduces freight charges, but also helps clear congested highways.

Since the new freight cars are so much larger and better than the old, they cost about twice as much. But they have roller bearings, improved springs, and cushion-type underframes, which make it possible to transport even fragile loads without the damage that

Even the steam locomotives were streamlined in recent years. *Milwaukee Road*

formerly was a part of freight handling. Larger doors on the cars, automatic hoists and elevators also help eliminate damage.

In 1968 mail cars were discontinued, and the carrying of mail given to the airlines, except for those communities that do not have air service. This seriously cut into the revenue of the railroads and was bitterly regretted by the owners. Still, in the interest of fast mail transportation, the change was liked by the general public.

But it is the locomotive that has seen the greatest change in the past twenty-five or thirty years. In June, 1887, a successful test run was made by a locomotive using oil for fuel instead of coal or wood. This was a passenger train that ran from Altoona to Pittsburgh, Pennsylvania, and back again. It was proved by this run that oil could be used as a fuel to heat the water in the boiler to make the steam which is the motive force of the engine. But nothing much was done with this knowledge.

A modern retarder control tower supplements the automatic slowing down of heavy freight trains. Weather and other conditions are fed into the electronic brain by the retarder operator. When it is necessary, he can take over manually. *Southern Pacific Company*

railroad, has gone. Today all sorts of modern equipment — steel cranes, power tools, magnetic eyes — are used to inspect cars and rails and to lay new ties and tracks where needed. Wonderfully equipped yards and shops are maintained at various cities. There cars and engines are carefully inspected, overhauled, reconditioned, or rebuilt. A modern locomotive weighs many tons, yet in a big, clean, well-lighted shop a huge crane will hoist it high, as if it were a toy, so that every underpart can be examined.

The old clickity-clack rails are being removed to be replaced by quarter-mile lengths of modern welded rails. Modern equipment and power tools do work that was once done by backbreaking labor. *Northern Pacific Railway*

A railroad yard today is an enormous complex of rails and switches. It is lighted at night by floodlights so that work can go on at all hours. This is especially true of freightyards, where cars must be shifted to make up a train for some distant city. The fast movement of freight is one of the necessities of today's world. People in cities and towns across the country can enjoy fresh fruits and vegetables and flowers from farms hundreds of miles away.

No longer does a stationmaster have to manipulate a highball signal by hand. Railroad offices, shops, and yards are equipped with all the latest devices for communication. Radio and loudspeakers are used to transmit orders. Closed-circuit television enables the operator in the control tower to examine the cars for the symbols that tell him what they carry and where they are going, so he can shunt each one to its proper place in a train that is being made up.

On the early trains there was no way for the engineer and the conductor to talk with each other. The first device used was rigged up by a conductor named Ayres on the Erie Railroad more than 100 years ago. Conductor Ayres tied a piece of wood to a string and hung this over the engineer's head. He carried the string back to his passenger coach. When he wanted to attract the engineer's attention, he pulled on the string, joggling the block of wood. Such a device could not be used on today's long, fast trains. Instead, these two important people communicate by radio and telephone. There is always radio communication between the front and the rear end of a train, no matter how long it is, between trains, and between trains and stations. Microwave radio towers transmit needed information on freight, weather, and track conditions.

The "Little Red Caboose," celebrated in song and story, has given way to this modern steel-sheathed room with two-way radio communications and many appurtenances for the comfort of the crew. *Great Northern Railway*

A traffic control room has a series of panels on which lights show the tracks and the positions of all trains in the yard. Sitting at his desk, the operator can see exactly where each train is, and he can move cars swiftly and safely to where he wants them. Such central control is absolutely necessary today when a dozen long trains may have to be shunted from track to track without accident.

An old railroad advertisement told people: "Steam engines used except in rainy weather. Then horses will be used." No such change is needed today, for weather scarcely ever stops a train. Still, weather poses problems. Blizzards in the northern part of the country pile snow on the tracks, freeze switches, and make rails slick. But the experiments through the years with various types of snowplows have paid off. Now a giant snowplow cuts right into the drifts and sends a long stream of snow into the air to fall beside the right-of-way.

An operator at the control board in the station routes the trains through the yard merely by pressing a button. Switches are thrown automatically so that no two trains can be sent over the same track at the same time. No longer any fear of being "asleep at the switch." *General Railway Signal Company*

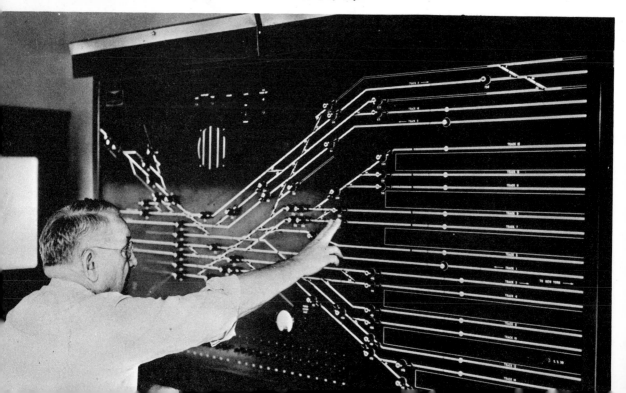

Automatic signals, half gates, and bells give warning at grade crossings. This one is at Wells Beach, Maine. *Boston and Maine Railroad*

At grade crossings on important highways, flashing signals warn that a train is approaching. Before the engine reaches the crossing, a long striped arm, or gate, is lowered to keep people off the track. On minor roads, signs warn people that a train may be coming. They should look carefully before crossing on foot or bicycle or in a car.

Major railroad companies maintain training schools for employees. The modern engine is so complicated a machine, communication so specialized, and even office work so technical that most employees must have instruction and training before they can handle their jobs.

Running trains is not the only concern of the large railroad companies. They advertise in many ways. They conduct visits for schoolchildren. They maintain libraries and photographic departments. Their research departments are constantly looking for new

The modern snowplow digs into the drifts and sends a great stream of snow through the air to clear the tracks. *Union Pacific Railroad*

and better equipment and methods. These departments have improved George Westinghouse's air brake, so that now the brakes can instantly stop the heaviest trains, even on steep downgrades. The iron of the rails has been tested and strengthened. Every bolt and every spring have been studied to learn the best way of treating the metal to make it strong and safe. Experts even study the tilt of the cars as they go around curves at high speeds, to make sure that this action is safe and comfortable. All sorts of fire retardants are tried out and the best ones used on the seat upholstery, drapes, and other flammable materials. There is so little danger of the fires that once cremated unfortunate passengers that fear of this particular danger is groundless.

Nevertheless, in spite of all precautions, accidents still happen. Late in 1968 there was trouble at Ashtabula, Ohio, where, in 1876, ninety-two people were killed when a bridge gave way, hurling a train 150 feet to the creek below. A more recent accident involved a runaway Penn Central freight train of sixty-five cars loaded with coal and drawn by five diesel engines. For some reason it was impossible to stop the speeding train, so the crewmen jumped before the first engine hit a curve and derailed the cars. One engine caught fire, all sixty-five cars overturned, but no one was seriously hurt.

In spite of what the railroad companies have done to keep abreast of modern transportation, the past fifty years have not been all rosy. Competition, labor troubles, and rising costs of material and labor all have done their part to plague the companies.

Many people who used to travel on trains now make their trips in their own cars. Highways and roads are getting better all the time, and a car allows freedom of movement impossible in any public con-

At a Purdue University laboratory a railroad brake shoe is tested at speeds up to 100 miles per hour. Research like this is giving the public safer, smoother train stops. *Association of American Railroads*

veyance. Modern buses have attracted millions of travelers, for both short and long rides. And today's speedconscious people have taken to airplanes in huge numbers. All these travelers once used the trains; the loss of their patronage has been hard on the railroad companies.

Labor troubles have not been especially bad for the railroads; still, they have caused problems. The first railroad strike occurred in 1877, during the golden age of steam, when the Baltimore and Ohio cut wages. This was a bitter conflict, with state troops and Regular Army regiments called out to break the strike. A number of workers were killed and many more injured. This outburst was followed by other strikes on the Pennsylvania and the Erie railroads. All these strikes were characterized by riots, destruction of property, and death. Baltimore, Pittsburgh, Buffalo, and Chicago were the hardest-hit cities.

The disastrous year of 1877 was followed by years in which less important walkouts disrupted train service here and there. The organizations of railroad workers known as brotherhoods were beginning to sponsor strikes as a weapon with which to gain benefits for underpaid and overworked employees. Then, in 1894, the great Pullman strike brought state and federal troops to Chicago and turned that city into a riot-torn camp.

By 1901 most workmen's groups had been organized into one union or another to carry on campaigns for better pay and better working conditions for their members. Most of the time they have won their demands through peaceful arbitration, rather than through strikes and violence.

The high cost of the raw materials used in construction of locomotives, cars, rails, and other equipment has eaten into the income the railroads obtain from passengers and freight. This has caused increases in passenger fares and freight rates. Smaller lines have been unable to meet the cost of new equipment or of renewing old apparatus. This has led to complaints from the public, who point to shabby, dirty cars as a reason for avoiding train travel.

Labor costs, too, have risen. A recent controversy has been over what is called featherbedding. The term refers to the demands made by the unions, and agreed to in the past by the companies, that many workers be paid when they are not actually working or for work they do not do. Such measures were adopted to protect the workers from wage losses caused by interruptions of their work, but they have come to be a nuisance and an expense.

Taking an overall look at the railroads today, one sees many improvements in equipment and operation, but some deterioration on the smaller lines. A number of obvious changes are being demanded by a public that wants speed, comfort, and convenience at the lowest possible cost. To some pessimists, the railroads are doomed to extinction, like the surrey with the fringe on top or the canalboat. Those who love the trains see in research, in electricity, in the diesel engine, a long future for rail travel and transportation.

18

RAILROADS OF TOMORROW

While some people are content to find fault with the railroads and to predict their imminent extinction, others are taking an active part in trying to preserve this valuable and interesting aspect of American life. The National Association of Railroad Passengers was organized by a Chicago attorney, Anthony Haswell. With about 2,500 members, this organization is working to get the federal government to take positive steps that will ensure the continued life of America's trains.

Chambers of commerce in various cities have taken up the crusade and have sometimes been able to prevent the discontinuance of a line that serves them. The railroad companies themselves issue booklets to schoolchildren, explaining what a train is and what it does. All this awakened interest may have an effect on the railroad of tomorrow.

Both America and the American way of life have changed

greatly since Peter Cooper's Tom Thumb raced a coach horse. And they are still changing, faster today than ever before. The population is increasing by leaps and bounds; farm products are being produced in ever greater amounts. The demands for electricity, housing, construction of all kinds are greater every day. All these trends have caused experts to say that by the year 2000 there will be an entirely new America. In a little more than thirty years the country will see as much new construction as it saw in all its previous history. This means that almost unbelievable loads of raw materials and finished products will have to be moved from place to place. In one month more people would have to use the trains than during the fifty years of the golden age of steam.

Railroad companies are aware of all this, and they plan to have a part in it. To do so, they know that certain changes must be made.

Among the people who want to see the railroads prosper are the model train buffs, like Daniel C. Jansen, an engineer on the Denver and Rio Grande. Thousands of model train builders are scattered over the country.

Steam railroad buffs work to preserve the "good old days of steam." Here drama students of the University of Chattanooga reenact the first trip of the Best Friend of Charleston, which took place on Christmas Day, 1830. The engine and cars are replicas of the originals. *Southern Railway System*

Neither the old Iron Horse nor the newer diesel streamliner can successfully compete with private cars and airplanes unless these changes are put into effect.

As far as the physical aspect of the trains is concerned, expert scientific researchers in laboratories and plants will be on the alert to discover and recommend adaptations and innovations. It is probable that more recreational features will be added to attract travelers. Many major lines already provide music, radio announcements, and similar features in passenger cars. A few offer television shows. In the future, such attractions will undoubtedly be increased.

The diesel, the gas-turbine, or the electric-powered engine is not the last word in locomotive development. Already there have been hints of nuclear-powered locomotives, whose possibilities are as yet unknown. But whatever the power that moves the train, it must be remembered that shining steel rails make transport easy, smooth, and fast. It is claimed that railroads, even today, can move three times as much freight per gallon of fuel as big trucks and eighty times as much as cargo planes. This indicates that there will be work for trains for a long time to come.

When it comes to people, it requires ten to twenty lanes of expressway to move as many people in automobiles as can be handled on one track of a double-track railway. Also, tracks can be laid underground and underwater to leave surface areas free for other purposes. This is especially important in congested industrial regions. Another advantage of trains is that they can travel in snow and fog. A Salt Lake City newspaper made a joke of this when the airport was fogged in for several days in 1968. An unhappy traveler grumbled, "You can complain as you will about trains, but I've never circled a railroad station for two hours, looking for a chance to land."

Double-deckers, built of stainless steel and carrying 148 passengers, have proved valuable in interurban service. This type of passenger car is an example of what will be seen on more trains of the future. *Association of American Railroads*

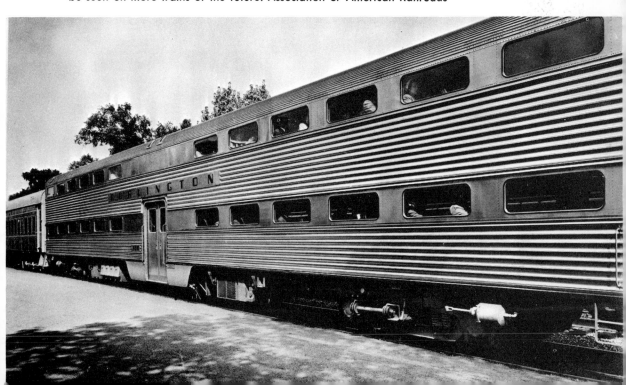

Because of the decrease in passenger travel, many passenger trains have been discontinued, and many more probably will be. In 1967 alone, 75 regularly scheduled trains were abandoned. In 1968 the Interstate Commerce Commission was asked to permit the stopping of another 108. Such petitions cause real concern throughout the area affected. There are hearings, letters to newspapers, local editorials, and so on — but not enough passengers to make the line pay. An example of this occurred recently in Utah.

In the spring of 1968 the Union Pacific asked the Interstate Commerce Commission to let it discontinue the passenger trains between Salt Lake City and Butte, Montana. Officials of Ogden objected, yet, when questioned, not one of them had ridden on this train for many years. Other Utah towns along the line also presented objections, but the Idaho cities involved sided with the railroad company, saying that to keep the passenger trains would cause freight rates to increase to make up the loss of revenue.

From such cases it appears that many little-used passenger lines will disappear from the railroad map of the country. Many suggest that even the major, long-distance lines stop trying to compete for passengers. For these companies, revenue is lessened because income from travel must be shared among several lines that cover approximately the same ground.

The railroad system of the country grew without any overall plan such as there probably would be today if a whole new system were to be laid out. Now the companies think they have the answer to this hodgepodge of tracks running every which way and often side by side. This answer lies in the merger — the combination of several lines in order to have a smaller number of systems. Money could then be put into providing better service at lower cost. Because railroads

This map shows the haphazard network of railroad lines that existed in 1966. More than 100 short lines have been discontinued, and further simplification is planned. *Association of American Railroads*

are still so important to the country, any such merger must have the government's approval. A merger involves a good deal of adjustment of tracks, equipment, and finances. Mergers have occurred during the past several years, and more seem ahead. A streamlined railroad system, with duplications and unneeded lines eliminated, seems to be one of the major changes of the future.

On October 15, 1966, an act of Congress created the Department of Transportation, a badly needed organization to help iron out some of the difficulties facing the railroads. This office will examine government policies toward the railroads and thus, it is hoped, modify such policies as seem unfair or which tend to hinder the full and best use of rail transportation.

Meanwhile, a great deal of research is being done on the construction of super-fast trains. Just as speeds of 50 miles an hour posed problems 100 years ago, so speeds of 125 to 150, now the aim of some lines, present difficulties. On a trial run of a super-fast train in Illinois in 1968, it was found that wheels and rails were unable to withstand the heat generated by such speed. Work is now being done to find a way to toughen the metal so it can meet the new requirements.

Mergers of two or more railroad companies are not the only simplifications foreseen. It has been suggested that a true transportation company of the future will combine the services of all modes of transportation of people and cargo — by road, rail, air and water. It is claimed that with one company handling cargo from its source to its final destination, time, energy, and cost would be reduced. Opposed to this idea is the dislike of monopolies and the love of competition. What can be done about it remains to be seen.

Some of the features of tomorrow's railroads are being tried out today. One of these is the clickless rail, which is replacing the 16-foot-long rail of the past, over which the wheels went clickity-clack as they passed the joining. The new rail is welded into one continuous strip that bends smoothly around curves, reduces upkeep, and provides safety against slipped joints that could cause derailment. Several thousand miles of this new track have been laid, and it has proved so worthwhile that it will doubtless be the rail of the future.

Experiments are also being tried with crossties of concrete, rather than wood. This looks like a throwback to the old stone crossties of the early New England railroads. The concrete, however, is made especially for this work; it will not break or split with use or with cold. New methods of securing the rails to the ties are being tried.

Perhaps you recall that the terrible accident involving the Hagenback-Wallace circus train was caused when the engineer stopped to repair a hotbox. Other accidents, from time to time, were due to the same difficulty: The bearings of the wheels became overheated, and the train had to be stopped to correct the problem.

The hotbox, or overheated axle bearing, has never stopped worrying the railroads, but in tomorrow's trains this difficulty should be eliminated. Since 1960, research has made great improvement in the bearings, and the work goes on.

Advances in communication are ahead. The TeleRail Automated Information Network (TRAIN for short) will establish a nationwide computerized system for tracking freight cars. This will provide up-to-the-minute information on the location of every freight train in the country at any given moment. Another system, Automatic Car Identification (ACI), will identify freight cars as they pass along. It will feed its information into TRAIN, so that freight car movements will always be known. This will speed up freight train movement and will give the control-tower operator the knowledge he needs to use the expensive freight cars more efficiently.

The railroad companies foresee four major areas in which the railroads will serve the country more competently than any other transportation medium: for service in and around congested big cities; in high-speed service along the stretched-out urban areas that are being created by our fast-growing population and between the cities along the Atlantic and Pacific seaboards; on certain scenic routes; and in time of war.

Demonstration programs are already being worked out by the railroad companies and the government to test the value of high-speed trains in the heavily populated strip from Boston to Washington. For such trains to operate effectively, there must be cooperation or mergers that will enable the trains to fly over the rails with a minimum of red tape and delay. Experimental double-decked commuter trains have proved especially adaptable to intercity service.

Other experimental trains are already being tried out. Early in 1969 the Penn Central Railroad's new Metroliner streaked from Washington to New York, inaugurating a new type of passenger service. Electric-powered and requiring no engine, the sleek silver coaches have the plush look of today's jetliners. Heavy carpets, wide, spacious seats, and many of the comforts and luxuries of planes make the trip comfortable, fast, and safe. This train can make up to 160 miles per hour but is kept to a speed of 120 miles or less, since roadbeds have not yet been built to withstand too great speeds. The trip from Washington to New York is made in less than three hours, at a fare about one-third less than airplane fare.

Another high-speed train is the gas-turbined Turbo-Train of the New Haven line, running between Boston and New York. This has a gleaming engine with no resemblance at all to the puffing black monsters of a few years ago. Constructed of aluminum by the United Aircraft Company, the Turbo-Train is capable of 170 miles per hour; it can round curves at high speed and so smoothly that a coffee cup filled to the brim will not slop over.

Added to the new speed and comfort of these trains is the fact that they come into the central part of the city, not to a distant airport.

The new high-speed trains have been developed under the High Speed Ground Transportation Act passed by Congress. This set aside $90,000,000 to finance demonstration projects, in the hope that the rails can attract passengers and so relieve the overcrowded highways and sky lanes.

From the time in the 1850's when a train would stop to let the passengers get out to view the landscape spread before them, railroads have proved an excellent method of seeing the country. In a private car the driver misses much because his attention must be focused on the road. This is especially true in mountainous country, where narrow roads and dangerous curves allow little opportunity for gazing at scenic wonders. Buses afford scant provision for observing the scenery, and airplanes fly too high. The observation car, especially the glass-domed, high-decked cars, are ideal for this purpose. There the traveler sits at ease on upholstered seats, high above the ground. He can see far and wide in absolute comfort and safety.

Especially interesting in this connection was an event that took place in the summer of 1967, when the Atchison, Topeka and Santa Fe added a new excursion train to its route. Although this line has long been known simply as the Santa Fe, it had no line to the capital of New Mexico. Passengers detrained at Lamy to take a bus to Santa Fe. But in 1967 a trial excursion train ran from Lamy to the capital with 225 enthusiastic passengers aboard. This strip of tracks, with S curves and 11 percent grades, is one of the most scenic in the entire state.

The Chamber of Commerce of Albuquerque organized a train task force to promote daily steam engine runs between Albuquerque and Santa Fe. Such encouragement may preserve a number of steam engines to supplement the business trains of tomorrow.

In any military or defense activity, the railroads have proved their versatility and value. Today there is a hot line between military and railroad officials that permits the trains to respond immediately to any demand that might be made or to any sudden emergency that might face the nation.

Most of the ammunition, gasoline, and heavy equipment sent overseas today is carried to the seaport by rail. Sulfuric acid, which is needed in ammunition, is carried only by rail. The heaviest tanks and missiles are carried by rail. The trains of tomorrow must be ready and equal to any emergency.

Railroad officials are optimistic compared to some of the public. In a talk before the National Press Club of Washington, D.C., a few years ago, Daniel P. Loomis, president of the Association of American Railroads, expressed this hopeful view. He spoke of the "Key to the super-railroads of America's future — to a railroad plant and train services right out of a dream — a dream . . . with real substance — which is already taking shape in stations, yards, control towers, offices and on rail sidings and mainlines all over America.

"Its form can be seen in whole trains of truck trailers riding piggyback on flatcars between our cities, in autos moving three deep from factories on special rack cars, in unit trains hauling massive loads of coal non-stop between mines and power stations, in push-button freight car classification yards, electronic train control systems, huge new types of hopper and tank cars and flashy long-haul passenger trains."

That, as well as anything, gives a picture of the railroads of tomorrow. As the California poet Joaquin Miller said: "There is more poetry in the rush of a single railroad train across the continent than in all the gory story of burning Troy."

Index

Stockton and Stokes stagecoach company, 27
Stourbridge Lion (locomotive), 20–22, 34, 72
Strickland, William, 15–16

Tank cars, 224–25
TeleRail Automated Information Network (TRAIN), 249
Texas, 124
Texas (locomotive), 91
Texas and Pacific Railroad, 117
Time zones, 146–47
Titusville, Pa., 171, 224
Toledo, Peoria and Western Railroad, 184–85
Tom Thumb (locomotive), 26–28, 51, 59
Topeka, Kan., 156
Torrington, Conn., 200
Tracks and rails, 12, 17, 20, 56, 57, 64–66, 232–33, 245; clickless rail, 248; curves of, 22, 26, 34, 43; gauge of, 52–53, 63–64, 118, 127; iron rails, 64–65; steel rails, 66; stone rails, 64; T rails, 65, 66; wooden rails, 20, 64, 65

Tracy, Harry, 211
Train robberies, 204–17
Transcontinental railroads, 64, 96–116, 117–26
Transportation Department, U.S., 247
Tredgold, Thomas, 17
Trevithick, Richard, 18
Trinidad, Colo., 129
Tunnels, 101, 105, 200
Turbo-Train, 250

Union Pacific Railroad, 64, 98, 99, 105–8, 111–16, 117, 129, 133, 209, 219, 246
United States Military Railway Service, 88, 94
Utah, 133–36
Utah Central Railway, 135

Van Buren, Martin, 160
Vanderbilt, Cornelius, 57, 149, 150
Vanderbilt, William H., 164
Virginia and Truckee Railroad, 136–39
Virginia City, Nev., 137, 138, 139

Wabash River, 75
Washington, George, 183
Watt, James, 12
Webb, Sim, 192, 193
Webster, Daniel, 53, 176
Wellington, Wash., 188
Wells, Henry, 167, 168, 169
Wells, Fargo and Company, 167–68, 169, 212
West Coast of Mexico Route, 125
Westinghouse, George, 42, 238
Wheeling, W. Va., 51, 71
Whistler, George Washington, 37
Whitman, Walt, 95
Williams, Ariz., 178
Winans, Ross, 43, 230
Woodbridge, N.J., 190
Wright, Archibald, 56
Wyoming, 97, 108, 111

Yerrington, Henry M., 138
Yonah (locomotive), 90, 91
Young, Brigham, 133, 135
Younger Gang, 207–9
Yuma, Ariz., 125

Zulu trains, 125–26

256